Do You Want to Save the Church?

A Handbook for Pastors and Lay People

Young J. Choe

Hamilton Books

An Imprint of
Rowman & Littlefield
Lanham • Boulder • New York • Toronto • Plymouth, UK

Copyright © 2017 by Hamilton Books
4501 Forbes Boulevard, Suite 200, Lanham, Maryland 20706
Hamilton Books Acquisitions Department (301) 459-3366

Unit A, Whitacre Mews, 26-34 Stannary Street,
London SE11 4AB, United Kingdom

All rights reserved
Printed in the United States of America
British Library Cataloguing in Publication Information Available

Library of Congress Control Number: 2016953959
ISBN: 978-0-7618-6862-0 (pbk : alk. paper)—ISBN: 978-0-7618-6863-7 (electronic)

∞™ The paper used in this publication meets the minimum requirements of American National Standard for Information Sciences Permanence of Paper for Printed Library Materials, ANSI/NISO Z39.48-1992.

Young Choe is often regarded as a 'critical thinker' and his penetrating pastoral writings continue to speak to us in twenty-first century. I read the chapters of this work as reflecting his loving passion for the ministry and for today's church. It is an important appeal on his part and that of others for a healthy and fruitful ministry. It reveals the stark reality of the current situation in the church and conveys the urgent need for greater participation and commitment to the church community.

The ministry belongs to no one, rather it is a conduit for God's engagement in everything.

Bishop Hee-Soo Jung, Ph.D.
United Methodist Church, Wisconsin Conference

Contents

Foreword: Why Do I Have to Speak Up?		vii
Notes		x
1	Every Church Is Struggling for Restoration	1
	A Deep Concern for the Decline of the Church	2
	Things Seem To Be Going Well Everywhere Except at the Church	4
	The Pastor Is Getting Sick in the Ministry	5
	The Statistics of Church Membership in the USA	6
	Notes	10
2	The Roots of Decline in the Church	11
	A Dialogue on the Current Trend	11
	Materialism as the Cause of Spiritual Desensitization	17
	The Institutional Church and the Status Quo	25
	The Church as a Stepping Stone	32
	Where Is the Church in the World Today?	34
	Socio-Ideological Issues	38
	Notes	39
3	Ten Reasons Why the Church Is Dying	43
4	Some Opinions on the Solution of This Problem	45
	Some Lessons from Experienced Pastors	46
	The Urgent Voices of Lay People	54
	Learning Leadership from the Business World	60
	Notes	67
5	The Sunday Pastor and the Everyday Pastor	69
	Who Is the Sunday Pastor?	70
	The Everyday Pastor Saves the Church	72

6	**The Healthy Lay and Church Disruptor**	75
	Conflicts Internal to the Church	76
	Group Games and Power Games	77
	Controlling Behaviors	77
	Unhealthy People as Rotten Apples	77
	Some Churches in Human Hands	79
	A Homogeneous Church	80
7	**Twenty Four Ideas for Restoring the Church**	81
	Mission Statement	81
	Some Programs That Can Affect a Turnaround in the Church	82
	A Proposal to the Board of Congregational Development	91
	Notes	94
8	**A Concluding Message on Saving the Church**	95
	Notes	102

Some Thoughts on the Church, Its Mission and Its Future　103
　Edgar Zelle

Bibliography　105

Foreword

Why Do I Have to Speak Up?

As a retired pastor of Wisconsin Conference of the United Methodist Church, I still have a burning desire to rescue the church from today's wave of decline. It is more serious than we think. And, if people deny this, then that only makes the problem still more serious, even desperate.

If your mother is seriously ill, what do you do? Do you take her to the hospital? Or do you keep her at home and care for her there? Or, if your

doctor says there is something wrong with your body, do you pay attention to what he says or not? If you are reluctant to listen to him or her, what will be happen to you later? Thus, if the church is sick, what are you going to do?

When we discover a problem in several areas of our lives, we will usually do a thorough examination of our situation. Let me give a personal illustration. I have been receiving dental care from Dr. Ross Werner of Randolph, in Wisconsin. He is a member of the Randolph United Methodist Church at which I have served. He not only cleans my teeth and gives a general checkup, but also uses x-ray to do a thorough examination. This is how a problem tooth was discovered.

Though I would like to keep my original teeth, the doctor explained that sometimes a defective tooth must be removed in favor of an implant. I appreciate the responsible approach of both of my doctors: Dr. Werner and Dr. Groethe. They are fully committed to taking care of their patients.

My wife has had a similar experience at Beaver Dam Community Hospital. In the emergency room, she received multi-medical technological care. Noting was found, however, since the staff as thorough they called the next day to re-check and to notify us that and there would be a follow-up test in three months. From this, I have learned that medical doctors and nurses are not reluctant to study the human body in close detail in order to protect us from dangerous diseases and that they promptly suggest action as needed.

Why should the Church be any different? If there is something not right in the Church, should we not make a diagnosis? If something is amiss, should we not get to the bottom of it? If a congregation is declining in numbers and worship attendance is low, should we not try to figure out why that is? Should we not take the opportunity to discuss such things in pastoral meetings and at church assemblies, conferences and workshops? Or, are we willing to live with the status quo until we have fallen off of the cliff?

According to historical records, the first ancient Olympic Games can be traced back to 776 B.C. they were closely linked to the religious festivals of the cult of Zeus, though not an integral part of any given rite. There is an interesting story relating to their origin. At one time, the ancient Greeks were threatened by an enemy who was trying to invade the land. A man took a torch in hand to light his way and he ran among the people to report the danger of war. According to this tradition, the Olympic Games were started to honor and celebrate this man's spirit.

Do we see anyone today, clergy or lay, who run in and out of our churches carrying torches and warning us of impending dangers? Where are the people who are addressing the decline of the Church? As a church leader, if I do work in the ministry again, I want to reflect the actions of a medical doctor who diagnoses carefully and does not hesitate to point up problems that exist. And, I want to see pastor and congregation working to restore the place of the church in the community.

Foreword

As for the church, I have a serious question. It is in the same position as the young person whose mother is sick. She needs to be taken to the hospital right away. A person who has a sick parent mother do their best to save her from any illness. In such a situation, we do not have time for coffee or for relaxing. She is facing a life or death situation. So is today's church.

In 2011 Fareed Zakaria and David Drehle participated in a roundtable discussion in a special edition of *Time* Magazine. In answer to this question of American decline, Zakaria stated on the cover page "Yes, America Is in Decline"; at the same time, David Drehle argued, "No America is Still No. 1."[1] As Zakaria insists, "Americans operate on the assumption that the U.S. is still No1." ("The U.S. is used to being No.1 . . .") and Drehle defends American prosperity: "...fallen trees don't prove the forest is dying."[2] But, we are rather warned of them as if to indicate that there is something dangerous going on in the forest.[3] If some of mountains are losing their trees in quantities, just planting a few new ones does not significantly help with reforestation. Instead, we have to correctly identify the bacteria or viruses which are infesting the trees.

For the reader, this book should be like the reading of an x-ray or the sounding of an alarm. It aims to carrying a torch, call for a rescue squad, and set a new of direction toward real solutions to these problems. We have spent millions of dollars to prop up a declining institution when our efforts should be redirected toward bringing life back into the church. It is for this reason that I have written this book—to help people refocus their efforts to at the serious and urgent work of saving the church. It is my hope that readers will derive from it a new and positive sense of direction that helps them to pull the church out of the ditch. We need a brilliant medical doctor who can both diagnose correctly and effect a long term and thorough cure!

The Jewish wisdom book, the Talmud, contains a great advice to parents on how teaching people how to catch fish rather than giving them money. I take this to be an appropriate metaphor for the situation I am discussing here as this book attempts to help church leaders and lay people to find a strategy for restoring the church in the midst of struggle and decline. The church needs roughly the same prescriptions as does the human body: healthy food, vigorous exercise, sufficient rest and a certain amount of social interaction. If this book offers the reader some useful guidelines for repairing the church and helping it move forward constructively, then it has served its purpose.

I also offer a metaphor for church leaders: I hope you look at yourself in mirror and ask if you would regard yourself as a trustworthy. Would you hire yourself to fix your broken car or cure your health problems, or solve financial problems?

My deepest appreciation goes to Bishop Hee-Soo Jung, United Methodist Church, Wisconsin, has suggested the title of this book, *Do You Want to Save the Church?* Also, I extend many thanks to the many pastors and lay people who have contributed their opinions and ideas for solution of this problem. This book is the product of their thoughtfulness, as it spans various denominations. We are on same page, struggling together against this decline and seeking viable and long-term solutions to it.

Thanks are also owed to Rev. Donald Zelle for his assistance and advising on this project. This book has come into being through the generous support of Sue Bentz, librarian of Moraine Park College of Wisconsin and my wife, Prisca. Finally I would like to dedicate it to my colleagues and readers in the hope that our combined actions can indeed restore the church to its proper place in society.

Young J. Choe
Lowell, WI 2016

NOTES

1. *Time* Magazine. March 14, 2011. Vol 177. No. 10.
2. Ibid. p. 34-35.
3. Young Choe, *Authentic Pastor, Authentic Leadership*. Lanham, MD. Hamilton Books, 2012. p. 12-13.

Chapter One

Every Church Is Struggling for Restoration

It is true that many of the churches are struggling for restoration in the midst of this decline. This is a chronic disease of today's church. Bishop Wilke, United Methodist Church, makes a tough statement in Chapter One ("Sick Unto Death") of his book, *And Are We Yet Alive?*:

> Our sickness is more serious than we at first suspected. We are in trouble, you and I, and our United Methodist Church. We thought we were just drifting, like a sailboat on a dreamy day. Instead, we are wasting away like a leukemia victim when the blood transfusions no longer work . . . Now we are tired, listless, fueled by the nostalgia of former days, walking with a droop, eyes on

the ground, discouraged, putting one foot ahead of the other like a tired old man who remembers, but who can no longer perform.[1]

Bishop Wilke's words reflect desperation. By 1986, he had already sensed the seriousness of the decline, hence his chapter title "Sick Unto Death." But, perhaps he is expressing himself too starkly? I would argue he is not. He is only telling the truth about this time period. He sees the situation correctly and has the appropriate level of seriousness about the problem. In fact, he sounds prophetic. However, today's church doesn't seem to listen to prophetic voices, either for its own benefit or that of the world. Instead, it wants to be lulled to sleep. But this indifference and refusal to take this situation seriously is leading to its emasculation and will eventually lead to its downfall. Without the prophetic voice, the church is blind. It actions can only be morally unsound and socially dangerous.

Also, Thom and Joani Schulz open their book, *Why Nobody Wants to Go to Church Anymore,* by stating, "There's no easy way to say this, but it needs to be said: The American church is broken."[2] I am as seriousness about this problem as they are. Accordingly, I offer my own assessment: Every church is either struggling for restoration, or on the way to its death. The death of the church means not only shrinking memberships, but also loss of a sense of commitment to core spiritual values. These developments make the church irrelevant to the world where Christian social responsibility is concerned.

Furthermore, this trend of decline is deepening dramatically in the mainline churches year by year. According to Steve Hewitt's report, "Every year, more than 4,000 churches close their doors compared to the approximately 1,000 new (and mostly very small) churches that start."[3] The healthy church is turning into a struggling one, and a struggling church soon becomes a dying one. In the end, it is trying to swim against a massive wall of floodwater, to survive in the midst of miserable conditions–and the result can only be closure of the church. At the conclusion of this process, all that will be left for the church supervisor to do is to wrap up paperwork for the closing. We see no significant changes occurring that would cause the church to turn around; no authentic leadership is coming to the fore to rescue it. So, if one church dies, the next will inevitably follow like a set of dominos. Therefore, I conclude that every church is struggling for restoration. In spite of this, however, I try to find the vision and direction necessary to keep the church afloat, to maintaining it properly. After all, it is the body of Christ.

A DEEP CONCERN FOR THE DECLINE OF THE CHURCH

In 2012, my book, *Authentic Pastor, Authentic Leadership* focused on church leadership as requisite to restoring and revitalizing the church in the midst of its decline. However, I have now decided to rewrite that book because I have observed that today's church is ever more seriously shaken and, in fact, vanishing. Why should I share this concern with you?

There are numerous religious and social reasons for doing so. First, according to St. Paul, (Eph. 1:23), the church the church is the body of Christ. This is his theological definition of God's presence through Christ and the Holy Spirit. The Christian church has continued to develop the human spirit and culture toward ever greater human freedom and so increasing secularization of its religious culture. But, if churches vanish, then the future of Christianity itself will be in doubt. And, Christian culture will be wrecked. What will replace it in the empty space that is created by its collapse should it occur? Probably churches will become like museums, mere collections of antiquities and galleries of past images. But, how can Christ be manifested in the world without the church? Is there a counterproposal being made anywhere?

Second, America was founded in conjunction with the church. For almost two centuries now, church and state have been working together like two sides of the same coin. The state provided the cement necessary to construct the foundation of the nation, and the church provided the water which enabled the cement to solidify. These two came together to form the concrete upon which the nation has been built, socio-politically and religiously. The church stood for moral values, clean and honest living. Many of the first Christian churches in the U.S. had good reputations. Churches and religious orders have built hospitals, schools, daycare centers, socio-cultural service centers, etc., and also carried out impressive work on behalf of love and justice. American churches have also reached out to take care of the world beyond their own shores. Korea is a case in point. Starting in 1950, life there was disrupted due to the Korean War. The country was basically reduced to ash. But Korea now has the seventh largest economy in the world. American missionaries helped it facilitate its turnaround. In fact, the American Church is still sending missionaries out to the entire world. America is a country in which the church has served and can continue to serve as a model to the world as far as religious traditions and their outreach programs are concerned. It can keep the world safe under the eyes of God. But, do we hear the voice of the church crying out on the street corners today? Asking the world to honor love and justice? Sadly, not. Instead, we see only increasing decline and ever fewer new churches.

In America, if the church disappears, the nation will be broken. It will have lost a central part of both its cultural and spiritual legacy and history. This is synonymous with the fall of a large axe upon American civilization. What will fill the spiritual emptiness that would be created by such a collapse? Will the nation manage to move forward without its churches?

If the church vanishes after this struggle, then the future society of America may be in doubt. Two outcomes can reasonably be predicted:

First, the words of 2 Timothy 3: 1-5 may be fulfilled:

> There will be terrible times in the last days. People will be lovers of themselves, lovers of money, boastful, proud, abusive, disobedient to their parents, ungrateful, unholy, without love, unforgiving, slanderous, without self-control, brutal, not lovers of the good, treacherous, rash, conceited, lovers of pleasure rather than lovers of God—having a form of godliness but denying its power. Have nothing to do with them. (NIV).

And, this prophetic word is not applicable only at a time in the distant future. There is already a trend toward serious social disorder and brokenness.

Second, if the trend of decline continues indefinitely, today's institutional church will disappear. A new Christian movement may arise. I can imagine a true Christian Kingdom movement without the institutional church in the future. However, I share the concerns of John Wesley on this point:

> I am not afraid that the people called Methodists should ever cease to exist, either in Europe or American. But I am afraid, lest they should exist as a dead sect, having the form of religion without the power.

John Wesley was a Methodist luminary who came from the Anglican Church. He was therefore able to predict the dead sect of institutional church today. So, why is this happening again? What is motivating it? What is the root and cause of the decline and whence all the brokenness?

THINGS SEEM TO BE GOING WELL EVERYWHERE EXCEPT AT THE CHURCH

It looks like everything goes well on Main Street. McDonalds is still functioning as is Burger King. Children still fill the kindergarten in the towns and villages as well as the school across the road. Business stores and restaurants satisfy people's desires. People are still seen coming and going on the streets. Government buildings and city halls are still up and running, taking care of their administrative responsibilities. Libraries help the people to learn and acquire information. But, why is the church struggling and suffering such a decline? Why is it disappearing? Why are churches closing? This is shameful!

In answer to this, someone might say that factories are closed and the population is moving out. Of course, a closed factory makes people who work at these jobs move into a new town. But young people especially are disappearing from the town as they look for jobs and go to college. However, even though a factory is closed, there are still people with children. And, someone else might say there are too many churches given the size of the community, too much competition for membership. Yet, on average, only 20–30% of the village people attend church on Sunday. The remaining 70% do not go to the church. The problem is that they are often invited by the church people. There are still some non-church people who are invited, but the church does not seem to have a vision for expansion, it has no activities in place for making disciples for Jesus Christ.

The world population is expanding rapidly, but, at the same time, that of many its countries is shrinking. However, the American population continues to grow and the country still offers some of the best conditions for raising a family. With the exception of a few geographic areas, America is still experiencing overall growth and vital demographic change.

If population loss and factory closings are not a decisive factor in the decline of the church, then what is causing it? We often say that everything is thriving except the church. We see still McDonalds, schools, businesses, stores, restaurants, etc. around the villages, yet, year by year, the church comes ever closer to disappearing. What is the underlying cause of this decline? Is it the pastor who is to blame or the congregation? At this point in time, this is a burning issue for me and for many others. In fact, it has motivated this writing.

THE PASTOR IS GETTING SICK IN THE MINISTRY

Recently, *Connections* magazine of North American Lutheran Church, carried an article on "Resurrection for Pastors" (2015) by MD Chavez. He claims unambiguously that the church is dying. In his words, "Churches in North America are in need of resurrection. Many factors have led to the decline. It is tempting to blame external factors, such as an increasingly secular culture that is in tension and sometimes opposition, with the Christian. However, churches have also contributed to the decline."[4] External factors, e.g., secular culture, humanism, atheism, other religions, etc. are not the cause of this decline; rather, it is being caused by significant internal factors such as the overall moral and ethical unhealthiness of clergy and the attitudes of the congregation.

Some findings from a Notre Dame study of Protestant clergy are as follows: 80% of male pastors' wives wish their husband had a different job; 20% of clergy are experiencing burnout; an additional 20% show signs of burnout; 46% of Protestant male clergy are obese. This latter figures is 10–13% higher than the national average. And, finally, 75% of Protestant male clergy have seriously considered leaving the ministry in the past year.[5]

According to Chavez, for several decades, the clergy, as a vocational group, have been among the least healthy people in North America, physically, mentally, and spiritually. But now they are identified as distinctly unhealthy. Therefore, he suggests that the lives of pastors need to be renewed.

Although Protestant pastors are becoming physically and mentally sick and constitute a high percentage of the obese population, obesity is under control in other sectors of society such as the military community and the community of medical professionals. Obesity and being generally out of shape are not attractive traits of leaders in any career field. But, the Christian community never seems to make an issue of this where their leaders are concerned. Still, in our time, obesity is not endorsed either personally or socially. It is a disease, and thus destructive to the body and to society as a whole–an enemy of life. Therefore, obese leaders are not ideal role models for the public. Unfortunately, the Christian community is reluctant take responsibility for such issues or attempt to control them. This itself is shameful!

MD Chavez also observes that the church is turning into jobsite or a vocational group. The appointed pastors are not interested in a serious calling to the ministry, nor is the institutional Christian community. A creative-minded person cannot find a place there. Pastors have to follow the Conference policy and Christian dogma, and, by doing so, most of them are, in fact, obstructing the development of the Kingdom of God. In short, the institutional church restricts pastors to conforming to the church culture and discourages them from truly following Jesus.

On the other hand, it needs to be acknowledged that some pastors begin their appointments lacking in proper qualifications and without a sense of leadership or any deep convictions about their vocational goals. Some of them just try to play the role. And also, there are many miserable conditions sometimes develop around pastors, sometimes even political conflicts. They exhausting them and deplete their spiritual resources. For this reason, many pastors seek a second career and leave the church. And, there is no the end to the process of decline once the culture of a community has turned negative.

This chapter has discussed the trend of decline in the church. I am not writing to make its leaders and people feel lulled to sleep, but rather to clarify what is actually going on with this process. Therefore, the next chapter will discuss the true causes of this decline.

THE STATISTICS OF CHURCH MEMBERSHIP IN THE USA

According to the US Census Bureau (2012), the change in membership from 1990–2008 in five major denominations including fundamental and nondenominational groups was as seen in Table 1.1.

This report finds that Catholic, Baptist, Pentecostal, and Nondenominational groups are still growing. What ensures this? Catholicism is still conser-

Table 1.1.

	1990	2001	2008 Estimates (1,000)
Catholic	151,225	159,514	173,402
Baptist	46,004	50,873	57,199
Methodist	14,174	14,039	11,366
Lutheran	9,110	9,580	8,674
Presbyterian	4,985	5,596	4,723
Pentecostal	3,116	4,407	5,416
Nondenominational	194	2,489	8,032

vative. It applies its fundamental doctrines against secular culture and does not seem to backpedal on its own tradition. Catholics consistently maintain a system of religious schools and social outreach agencies and this perhaps contributes to the stability in their membership. It may even encourage the creation of new congregations. There is also the continual large influx of Catholics from across the southern U.S. border, and the concomitant lack of a prohibition on birth control. However, the current scandal and crisis of priest sexual abuse could negatively impact on growth of membership.

By contrast to this, Methodists and Lutherans are facing a decline in membership, though Pentecostal and Nondenominational groups are growing unexpectedly. Methodist, Lutheran, United Church of Christ, Presbyterian, etc. are well defined as concerns their doctrines and social principles. They have the proper biblical, theological, and social-ethical foundations in place. Among the mainstream churches, they therefore make a good impression. But they are behind Pentecostal and Nondenominational where growth is concerned. They may be suffering some decline due to their openness to homosexual marriage, though it is difficult to assess this at this point. Also, where membership is concerned, liberals are lost to the churches more often than conservatives. The Methodist church has still not addressed the homosexual agenda at the General Conference. However, they are losing membership constantly. They have money and a powerful system and institutional structure in place. What is the cause of this ongoing loss? Can we be hopeful about the mainline churches? Are they eventually on the way to their death? And, will they be replaced by new church movements? According the Prof. Thomas C. Oden, author of *Turning around the Mainline* (2006), the United Methodist Church has been in trouble for a long time. He observes that mainline churches stand today not merely in a crisis numbers, but in a deeper crisis of faith. This is often portrayed as a crisis of politics or demographics or moral values or sexuality, but it is more clearly one of biblical authority and relates to theological integrity. Rob Renfroe, publisher of *Good News*, also discusses this issue at length in his editorial "The Roadblocks to Our Future."[6] We are, without a doubt, in a serious crisis. But how much attention is it getting from the people as a whole?

In America, the United Methodist Church is the second largest denomination among the nation's Protestants. According to the reports of Douglas Johnson and Alan Waltz, it has been shrinking considerably in membership year by year. The following represents membership and average attendance at worship from 1965 to 2000

Tables 1.1 and 1.2 differ from those of the 2012 US Census Bureau. The Census reported the UMC membership (in 100s) at 14,174 in 1990; 14,039 in 2001; 11,361 in 2009. These are larger numbers than those reported by Johnson and Waltz. Nevertheless, the two Methodist researchers and US Census Bureau agree that there has been a steep drop in UMC membership from year to year.

Furthermore, the United Methodist church is in a crisis as concerns this declining membership. According to the Board of Discipleship, in 2009 the UMC lost 1,500 members per week across all of the US states. In 2013, approximately 300,000 were lost. Wisconsin Conference UMC Superintendent Sam Royappa reported in 2008 that the current membership throughout the entire state is 86,000 and everyday an estimated 9.2 members disappear. In the last fifteen years, we have lost more than 30 churches here in WI conference, average of two per year. In 2012, he predicted that if this trend continues, 103 churches would be closed within the next eight years. By this calculation, all of the Wisconsin Methodist churches would be closed by 2049. Accordingly, by 2050, the UMC would no longer be able to offer professional positions.[9]

This report points to the conclusion that the decline in the UMC membership is such that it will likely lead to the closing of the church in the future. In

Table 1.2.

Year	Membership	Attendance
1965	11,024,253	4,381,161
1970	10,671,774	3,853,703
1975	9,995,107	3,620,995
1980	9,545,445	3,547,033
1984	9,225,738	3,549,347
1986	9,106,764	3,451,463
1990	8,859,868	3,357,889
1996	8,489,524	3,217,529
2000	8,242,628	3,123,956

The Wisconsin Conference alone, 103 churches have disappeared over the last ten years. This is essentially a prediction of certain death for the institutional church as John Wesley established it.

Liza Kittle, the President of the Renew Women's Network, reported that the United Methodist Women membership also continues its dramatic decline. She compared data on membership for the United Methodist Church and United Methodist Women from 1974 to 2010.[7]

As she observes, this information is hardly a cause for joy. It is indeed heartbreaking to see that the church is in crisis. But this is not only happening in United Methodist Church. It is also a pronounced trend in the mainline churches. And why? Many other institutions are developing positively all around the world. So, why is the church not among them? Do you have an idea how to lessen this decline or slow it down?

Before closing this section, I would like to cite from a very recent report entitled, "Study Points out Decline" by Thomas A. Lambrecht in *Good News*. Where the collapse of Christianity in the United States is concerned, the Pew Research Center found that it had decreased from 78.4 percent of the population in 2007 to 70.6 percent in 2014. He further continues to describe the mainline church in the same terms:

Non-Christian faiths grew by 1.2 percent points to encompass near six percent of the population. But the big news was the jump in unaffiliated persons from 16.1 to 22.8 percent of the population, a growth of 6.7 percentage points Atheists and agnostics grew from 4.0 percent to 7.1 percent of the population. As an aside, United Methodists went from 5.1 percent in 2007 to 3.6 percent in 2014.[8]

Thus, we are still not seeing the end of this decline. How long will it continue?

Lambrecht comments on the reason for this in one of his subtitles: "It has become less necessary to identify oneself as a Christian in order to fit into our society."[9] This means that the church is no longer interesting to people, nor does it exert an influence on their lives. It is also apparently not having much effect on people in our technocratic society. Indeed, the Christian culture and its value are on the wane.

This chapter has discussed the trend of decline in the church. I am not writing to dull the sensibilities of church leaders and community members,

Table 1.3.

	UMC	UMW	Church Membership
1974	9.91 Million	360,000 (25% Decl.)	8,942
2010	7.57 Million	570,200 (58% Decl.)	33,346

but to identify the real cause of this problem and suggest solutions to it. The next chapter will therefore focus on the true causes of this decline.

NOTES

1. Richard B. Wilke, *And Are We Yet Alive?* Nashville, TN. Abingdon Press.1986. p. 9.

2. Thom & Joani Schultz, *Why Nobody Want to Go to Church Anymore,* Carol Stream, IL. Tyndale House Publ. 2013. p. 5.

3. Steve Hewitt, *Why the Church Is Dying in America,* in *Christian Computing Magazine*, July 2012, p. 3.

4. Mark Chavez, *Connections*. Maple Lake, MN. 2015. p. 37.

5. Ibid. p. 37

6. Rob Renfroe, *Good News*, July/August 2014, Woodlands, TX. p. 2. Prof. Oden taught at Drew University in the areas of theology and ethics.

7. Kittle discusses this in "UMW Membership Continues Dramatic Decline," in *Good News,* The Woodlands: Scriptural Christianity, March/April, 2012. pp. 26-27.

8. Thomas A. Lambrecht, "Study points out Decline," in *Good News*, July/August, 2015. p. 26.

9. Ibid. p. 27.

Chapter Two

The Roots of Decline in the Church

A DIALOGUE ON THE CURRENT TREND

Decline is a common and serious issue in the mainline churches in America. It is not only a matter of crisis, but also a chronic malady. The issues relating to it are not only a part of the physical disruption of the church, but also amount to a shaking of the spiritual foundations of our society, culture and religion. Such decline could foster a problematic American future in an instable society. What will replace in the emptiness of the church? And how do we cope with spiritual panic?

Between 1986 and 1987, two books were published by Abingdon Press of the United Methodist Church: *And Are We Yet Alive?*" by Bishop Richard Wilke[1] and "*Facts & Possibilities*" by Douglas Johnson and Alan Waltz.[2] These authors are worried about the future collapse of the church. They warned readers that church memberships were disappearing dramatically. As Bishop Wilke states, "During one period of great growth, the 1880s, 1890s, and early 1900s the denomination had twice as many people attending the church schools as were members of the church."[3] However, United Methodist Church had already begun to decline as early as the 1960s. Half of the church school vanished from 1960 to 1980. And, as he observed, the "rose-colored glasses no longer protect us from the facts."[4] In his view, it is hard for us to be optimistic about the future of the church.

The eloquent message of Bishop Wilke continues, "...Our great danger is that we cannot even turn ourselves around. We do not produce because we are improperly focused. We are like modern couples who decide not to have children because they want to find themselves."[5] I have a similar metaphor to offer. Today's church is like a hen which is not able to produce eggs. For this reason, Bishop Wilke called mainline denominations "old-line."[6] However, I say that the old-line is now "dead line" or "death-line." And, the problem is becoming deeper and more insoluble day by day.

These two books were published about 30 years ago, but what has happened since the turn of the millennium? The declining trend still continues—now even more seriously. In fact, the church seems like a patient who has a severe illness and is on the way to an intensive care unit.

In 2003, Reggie McNeal, Director of Leadership Development, South Baptist Convention published *The Present Future*.[7] His work offers a vision for turning the church around. He asks six tough questions: First, he states that the "North American church has substituted its own charter for a sort of clubhouse, it has become a place where religious people just hang out with others who think, dress, behave, vote, and believe like them. Furthermore, people who are just filling church jobs are contributing to its decline."[8]

McNeal also claims that the collapse of the church culture is the new reality number one:

> ... The church established by Jesus will survive until he returns. The imminent demise under discussion is the collapse of the unique culture in North America that has come to be called "church" ... In reality, the church culture in North America is a vestige of the original movement, an institutional expression of religion that is in part a civil religion and in part a club where religious people can hang out with other people whose politics, worldview, and lifestyle match theirs. As he hung on the Cross Jesus probably never thought the impact of his sacrifice would be reduced to an invitation for people to join and to support an institution.[9]

Thus, he predicts that the church of Jesus will move into the postmodern world in this fashion. This phenomenon has been noted by many who tag the emerging culture as post-Christian, pre-Christian, or postmodern. There is the real possibility that the church will become reduced to a community fellowship center or cultural center. Accordingly, I conclude that the institutional church is one of the causes contributing to the death of the church culture. Still, McNeal believes that the church established by Jesus will survive until he returns.

Secondly, he talks about *a refuge mentality* among church people which keeps the church out of the world. He states how this mentality badly affects the Christian view of the world:

> ... Those with a refuge mentality view the world outside the church as the enemy. Their answer is to live inside the bubble in a Christian subculture complete with its own entertainment industry. Evangelism in this worldview is about churching the unchurched, not connecting people to Jesus. It focuses on cleaning people up, changing their behavior so Christians can be more comfortable around them. Refuge churches evidence enormous self-preoccupation. They deceive themselves into believing they are a potent force.[10]

For this reason, there is a deep gulf between the church and the world. He insists that "people outside the church think church is for church people, not for them." Today's church stands for those inside the church. Sadly, it is becoming profoundly separated from the world, even though Jesus came into the world to heal it.

McNeal offers another reason as to why people are leaving the church. He talks about the church as *the club house* as follows.

> ... In their mind, the church is a club for religious people where club members can celebrate their traditions and hang out with others who share common thinking and lifestyles. They do not automatically think of the church as championing the cause of poor people or healing the sick or serving people ... They believe the church is out for itself, looking out more for the institution than for people.[11]

If such a trend is really developing, then the club church will prove to be only a dead sect, hardly the offspring of John Wesley's vision. The substance of ministry will dissipate in the clubhouse setting. And, there is no doubt that the institutional church is turning into a cultural center.

Even though the people are turning away from the church, they are not turned off to Jesus. Jesus is popular. Thus, some of the South Korean Christians say that they have to leave the church to keep their true faith. They find corruption and immoral behaviors inside the church. This case makes us recall Jesus' criticism that the Temple had become a den of thieves.

In McNeal's view, this trend of decline has been caused by a process of secularization, by a refuge mentality, and by the fact that the church has come to be viewed as a social club. In conclusion, the church is losing contact with the substance of its mission, it is abandoning the search for Jesus' Kingdom on earth. Therefore, McNeal suggests that redemptive efforts are necessary to save the world. His final words sound prophetic, "Trouble is, the church is sleeping on the job. Too many of us have forgotten why we showed up for work."[12]

In 2012, Abingdon Press published *10 Temptations of Church* by co-author, John Flowers of San Antonio and Phoenix and Karen Vannoy, District Superintendent. The goal of this work is to determine why churches decline and what can be done about it. The authors identify several reasons for this and outline ten temptations which are contributing to it.

First, the decline results from abuse of power. "A church that succumbs to temptations . . . is a "needy" church. Needy churches are about as magnetic as needy people. A church that succumbs to temptation quickly loses its way and forgets its purpose."[13] Such a church is no longer attractive to incoming members.

The book further discusses this decline as resulting from power games. "Declining churches resist changing their structure, and their leaders have roles mapped out in order to maintain the church's status quo, even amid decline."[14] They are struggling with leadership and proper allocation of office space in every area of the church community. They are also struggling conflicts between old and new-timers concerning expectations and accountability with respect to appointments. Some of the gifted leaders are not ready to serve the church spiritually. And also, they are struggling with a proper understanding of civic and spiritual leadership.

In the name of Christ, the church is not a place to practice power games. It is a divine community in which people are called to serve God for the betterment of the world. Power games make it possible for people to give in to their own desires and to act against God's will. So, the temptation to acquire and misuse power fosters decline.

Second, this book deals with financial depression and anxiety as a cause of decline. The authors find that "many declining churches haven't been able to grow their churches for so long they have lost faith in their ability to succeed at anything, much less a financial drive."[15] However, we need to remind ourselves that self-improvement comes before money management. Money is the outcome of faith at the church, not the cause of it. And also, Flowers and Vannoy find that as a church declines, it tends to depend on only a few individuals for the greater part of its financing. This disparity can make that the power of a single individual enormous under any circumstances. Whether it is large or small, however, an offering belongs to God alone. And, no amount of money can control Him. Instead, it is handled by Him.

Thirdly, as these authors note, the declining church is struggling with transitions in leadership. Consider, for example, a church secretary who had served for a long time. She complained that the nominating committee was trying to bring new people into the leadership. Evidently, she couldn't adjust to the loss of personal power. Some folks make it a point to stop by each Sunday and catch up on the latest news and gossip when they meet in the parking lot. They are tempted by the power of information.[16]

Fourth, a declining church faces the temptation to maintain status quo. When these authors were appointed to their first urban church, they found, to their astonishment, that the forty-year-old bulletins were not different than the current ones.[17] Worship should be central to changing the status quo. But changing worship patterns is a very sensitive issue and people tend to form "yes" and "no" groups. Sometimes, it even becomes a cause of church conflict and so contributes to decline. Change means re-creation and revitalization. However, a declining church is effectively being eaten away by its adherence to status quo.

Fifth, this book discusses "insider temptation" and the insider mentality. Such congregations need to feel intimate with each other. They insist that the church remain just as it has always been: "These congregants generally have a high need for stability and security of an unchanging church."[18] But, a homogenous congregation and a racist church do not make for a healthy community. There is no a place for Jesus to welcome people there. There is no "open door" for people who are seeking to the Kingdom of God. If the church segregates itself from the community, in this way, it will eventually disappear.

Sixth, the declining church is struggling between growing and shrinking where membership is concerned. For instance, "if a local church is growing, there is pressure to learn new names. This pressure makes us uncomfortable. We all know learning new names means we care. However, if the local church is in decline, it is easier to care for people . . . If a church is growing, we look for our friends on Sunday and miss them in a sea of new faces."[19] Under such conditions, there is no productive desire to improve the ministry. Exclusivity means inflexibility and so the inability to adjust to and embrace new faces.

Seventh, these authors observe that "Several teens and parents in this particular local church don't seem interested in growing the youth group, but they are powerfully tempted to maintain the youth scholarship program . . ."[20] In this case, a limited church budget needs to cover scholarships for youth and children. It is a burden for the church to continue the youth programs.

Eight, the declining church does not try to remember the names of new persons. It has pastors and staff who feel it a burden to make sure names, addresses, email addresses, telephone numbers, visitation, and so on are kept track of. Such laziness is therefore also a mark of a declining church. People are focused on the outside, on their secular jobs that run from 9 to 5. Se they take seriously for purely practical reasons.

Finally, this book deals with "The Temptation to Avoid the Hard Work of Assimilation" and "The Temptation: Play It Safe."[21] In declining churches, most of the pastors do not try to change the status quo. Change has become the enemy of church members over the last forty years. Flowers and Vannoy cite many reasons why the churches are declining, the most important of them being a failure to give priority to leadership.

In 2013, *The Great Evangelical Recession* was published by John Dickerson, a senior pastor of Cornerstone (Evangelical Free Church) in Prescott, Arizona. He discusses the fact that church membership is shrinking and sees this trend as being rooted in a sort of spiritual recession. He is concerned with how we can avoid a devastating collapse. He illustrates the collapse of the church in terms of six trends.

First, the Evangelical church is not an exception where decline is concerned. Both the size and the value of the church have long been overestimated. But, it is shrinking like the American economy. In his view, its decline is due to cultural changes, the baby boom, and so on. As he says, "We are no longer as mighty as we once were."[22] The Evangelical church is losing influence in the modern American secular culture.

Second, the oak of evangelicalism in America is struggling with both pro-homosexuality and anti-Christian reactionism. It is struggling to maintain traditional values in a radically changing society.[23] The two are at odds with each other.

Third, accordingly, hate creates division. Evangelicals will either assume a bunker mentality and allow the movement to drift into pluralism, or they will resist these changes and purify it in a spirit of grace and love. In 2004, the Evangelical group was identified as 48% of rightist, evangelicals and traditionalists; 41% of moderate and middle; 11% of leftist or modernist.[24] They continue to be divided over politics, theology, and practice.

Fourth, Evangelicals are experiencing the passing of the generation that are their most generous donors. The percentage of Americans who tithe and support evangelical works continues to decline. "Seventeen percent of Christians say they tithe—but only 3 percent actually give 10 percent or more of their income to the Lord's work."[25] If the church needs money, it has to touch people's hearts, move them to be generous.

Fifth, Evangelicals are losing the membership and so bleeding dramatically. They lose an estimated 26,000 every year. "Of the 3.7 million United States evangelicals who are eighteen to twenty-nine years old, 2.6 million will leave the faith at some point between their eighteenth and twenty-ninth birthdays."[26] This means that 712 disappear every day. This is a trend that is due more to lack of proper maintenance of the church community than to direct attention to membership. Jesus called His followers to make disciples, but today's church focuses instead on internal politics.

Dickerson concludes that the church is sputtering in a wave of secularism. Where Jesus said "Take care of my sheep," he claims that we have failed to take care of Christ's sheep, by which he means that the Christian church has lost contact with the substance of the Gospel.

Even though our great prophets, Bishop Richard Wilke (1986) and Reggie McNeal (2003) have warned of the church's decline, today's church is still seriously struggling and, in fact, dying. A number of prophets have made valuable suggestions for reversing this trend. But we are still not seeing the desired reversal. As we know, the church grew and expanded from the 1880s to 1990s in America. But later it began to decline— never to recover its initial momentum.

Before concluding this discussion, we need to focus attention on another work, namely, *Why Nobody Wants to Go to Church Anymore,* by Thom and Joani Schulz. There provide four reasons why the church is declining: "a) I feel judgmental, b) I don't want to be lectured at, c) the church people are a bunch of hypocrites, d) your God is irrelevant to my life. But I'd like to know that there is a God and that he cares about me."[27] These points, as causes for decline in the contemporary church, are well examined by the authors. It makes a sense to learn about how the church itself is contributing to this decline.

Today, decline in the church is a trend that spans denominations in America. The church is in the world, but separated from it. In fact, both are becoming dissociated from each other. In this section of their work the authors conclude that a refuge mentality has created a deep gulf between the church and world. The declining church clings to the status quo and sees change as an enemy. The laziness of its leaders and their effective political and institutional emasculation contribute to the problem. And there does not seem to be any decisive way of setting in motion the necessary turn around. Instead, it is like people are just staring into a fire that is burning across the river. And also, the wave of secularism is becoming ever stronger than Christian values. As noted, the church is turning into social and cultural center, a sort of club house, and a mere human community rather than striving to become a divine one. These problems and trends are the root causes of the decline.

MATERIALISM AS THE CAUSE OF SPIRITUAL DESENSITIZATION

This section attempts to show how materialism has also contributed to this problematic decline in the church. It identifies and discusses the antagonistic relationship between spirituality and materialism in the American life style.

Process philosophers, even the Pre-Socratic thinker Heraclitus, claimed that "Everything is flux." Buddhists discuss this as well is the context of their focus on emptiness and dependent origination. Philosophers are generally curious about true and unchanging being. The ancient Greeks used the term *arche* to mean a source or point of origin of all being.

Thales, one of the earliest of the Pre-Socratics, claimed that *water* is the basis of all things. He regarded is as the most fundamental form of being. Empedocles says there are four principles: *water, fire, air*, and *soil* and these serve as the origin of the world. Democritus says the invisible *atom* which is true being. On the other hand, Heraclitus claims that the *Logos* as the unchangeable principle of things. Plato takes *Ideas* to be eternal. Finally, Christian philosophy says God is the sole eternal being. So, history has produced a mix of idealist and materialist theories where the problem of a first principle is concerned.[28]

After the ancient philosophers, the original home of modern materialism from the seventeenth century onwards, is England. Duns Scotus, a British schoolman, effectively made theology yield to materialism. And, modern philosophy declares that Bacon is the real progenitor of English materialism. He believed that science could save the world. Karl Marx wrote about the British origin of materialism.[29] However, both he and Engels are known to have championed materialism.

What exactly is materialism? Webster's Dictionary defines as follows:

a. The purely philosophic doctrine that matter is the only reality and that everything in the world, including thought, will, and feeling, can be explained in terms of matter (as opposed to ideas in the mind),
b. the political and social doctrine that comfort, pleasure, and wealth are the only or highest goals or values. The tendency to be more concerned with material than with spiritual or intellectual goals or values.[30]

Thus, materialism is interpreted 'matter' true being, not spirit. For the materialist, there is nothing but matter in the world—and, in the case of the atomists, atoms. This is diametrically opposed to the belief that the world was created from nothingness by God. Therefore, matter is the only value, and the end goal of all natural processes. It is also the only defining criterion of life, and the only visible reality–indeed it is viewed by materialists as true being. There is no place in such a schema for spirit or ideas. And, in a more mundane and socio-political sense, matter and material goods are the only a goal of life–comfort and pleasure, the ultimate rewards.

In ancient Greek philosophy, Leucippus and Democritus came to be known as fathers of materialism. Where Roman philosophy is concerned, the poet-philosopher Lucretius (BC. 95-52), held human's heart and spirit to be material. In his view, even soul consisted of matter because it was born of it. It is comes and goes like a plant. It is a process of nature and natural processes shape and define everything. Therefore, dying is nothing to worry about.[31] He sounds a bit like a modern materialist where this line of thought is concerned. And he is able to overcome the fear of death in an odd and circuitous way. If there is only one true being, it is matter, and matter itself has a kind of eternality.

Contemporary theologian Wayne Stumme proposes that materialism is opposed to the spirit of Christianity. In the nineteenth century, Karl Marx was a great champion of materialism, though of the more practical sort. He is a towering figure where a materialistic understanding of history is concerned as the following makes clear.

For the socialist, the whole of what is called world history is nothing but the creation of man through human labor, and the emergence of nature for man. Marx therefore has the evident and irrefutable proof of his own self-creation–in materialist terms.[32]

Marx is provocative where human work and society are concerned. "For him, the study of history became a weapon in the struggle for a radically different society . . . he offered the working class a revolutionary program. History is the story of a process of social and material development. The outcome of this historical movement was a profound and humanizing transformation of society . . ."[33] For this reason, Stumme states that Marx had repudiated "the belief that history was guided by the divine will and subject to divine intervention." In Marxism, the human being is only matter, only the subject in the creation of history. He removes the spiritual element from life and ignores divine intervention altogether.

Marx insists that human connection is based on materialism. "Thus, it is quite obvious from the start that there exists a materialistic connection of men with one another, which is determined by their needs and their mode of production, and which is as old as men themselves."[34] On his understanding, then, human relationships derive from behavior that is conditioned according to material desire.

Also, he insists that humans can be liberated by material achievement, because liberation is an historical, not a mental or a spiritual act. In essence, for Marx, there is absolutely no place for the workings of the spirit in human history.

Furthermore, he claims Marx that consciousness and language are social products. " . . . consciousness was formed in accordance with the way that persons organized their necessary productive activity. Different forms of consciousness—such as religion, philosophy, ethics, law, and art—had as their determining *basis the real process of production.*" In his view, these can only be defined in terms of economics. He insists that consciousness does not develop independently of its defining economic conditions. However, he doesn't seem willing to take account of the fact that spiritual forces are sometimes at work in people's overcoming poverty.

Also, Marx insists that the ideas of the ruling class are based on material forces. " . . . The ruling ideas are nothing more than the ideal expression of the dominant material relationships, the dominant material relationships grasped as ideas; hence of the relationships which make the one class the ruling class, therefore, the ideas of its dominance."[35] Thus one can conclude that he take the material to be the ruling force in history. He seems to know only the phrase, "money = relationships" in a capitalistic society, and not to recognize that the spirit is the ruling force in the human body and in the larger schema of history. This is, in effect, a tragic assessment of the human condition, one that is based in ignorance of God's creation. He totally ignores, or was perhaps unaware of, the relation between body and soul.

Religion was, for him, nothing but the opiate of the masses. As he says,

> For Germany, the criticism of religion has been largely completed; and the criticism of religion is the premise of all criticism . . . The basis of irreligion criticism is this: man makes religion; religion does not make man . . . The struggle against religion is, therefore, indirectly a struggle against that world whose spiritual *aroma* is religion . . . Religion is the sigh of the oppressed creature, the sentiment of a heartless world, and the soul of soulless condition. It is the opium of the people.[36]

His criticism of religion is notorious. And, it is based on that of Feuerbach, a radical German philosopher of mid-nineteenth century. As he says,

> . . . Feuerbach argued quite simply that belief in God was an alienating illusion created by human beings in response to their own fears and desires. God was nothing other than a human creation, an illusory being who, believers imagined, could rescue them from the fears and disappointments which plague human life . . .[37]

Thus, Marx reduces God to an illusion. The reason why human beings depend on God is that they are finite, constantly experiencing themselves as limited, weak, and incomplete. However, Marx has tried to liberate us by presenting God as illusionary.

Feuerbach also talks about a God who alienates human beings against humanity. Belief in God is destructive of human self-esteem. His own negative concept of God is as follows.

> . . . If God was the source of all that is powerful and good, then human beings had to be conceived as weak and lacking in good. If every positive quality was assigned to God, then we have only negative properties to assign to ourselves. Our exaltation of God becomes a denigration of humanity. Moreover, by conceiving of ourselves as dependent upon an all-powerful being we become

passive and inactive, failing to take responsibility for our own lives. *Belief in God was in Feuerbach's eyes the key to all human alienation.* We have taken our own good qualities—love, compassion, trust—and assigned them to an alien being, a being who is *wholly other . . .* [38]

Feuerbach clearly aims to define religion in destructive terms. Belief in God is a denigration of humanity and makes for human alienation. If religion itself does not bear responsibility for our condition, it can be blamed for it according to the Bible, Ezekiel 13: 6-9: Sometimes religion misleads people into blind behaviors makes them slaves to the institutional church. It preaches about the other world and neglects social responsibility in this world. Sigmund Freud "found no reason to believe in God and therefore saw no value and purpose in the ritual of religious life."[39] As he states, "religious ideas do not come from a God or gods, for gods do not exist . . . is certain that religious beliefs are erroneous; they are superstition...there is a close resemblance between the activities of religious people and behaviors of his neurotic patience . . ."[40] Thus he has blamed religion for making people immature and dependent upon it. All the religions that proceed in such a way must be blamed, because this is opposed to humanization. It is true that there are some religions that help people to resist such dehumanization as Feuerbach described.

However, Feuerbach failed to understand the true image of God as love and peace. He was ignorant in the difference between God and religion. God never changes–his love and justice are constant. Yet, institutionalized religion has indeed played a part in obscuring and manipulating the image of God. It is undeniable that there are some aspects of it that are morally questionable and have developed incorrectly. Still, there is a difference between the substance of the Christian teachings and the mistakes that have been made by the institution over time. On the other hand, if religion is reluctant to take serious responsibility for directing people's lives, then it is true that *belief in God* does alienate us from ourselves. In this respect, Feuerbach is right to claim that the death of religion would bring about emancipation.

He constantly claims that "religion opposes all those forces which bring about human misery and suffering"; in other words, *"religion is protest against real suffering."* But, I would argue that, by contrast to this, religion seeks the solution to human suffering in the spiritual realm. Maybe Feuerbach has erroneously claimed that both the problem and the solution to suffering lay in the material conditions of life. —and thus blocked all paths to emancipation: ". . . religion could never be more than *the sigh of the oppressed creature*; it could never become a resource for overcoming oppression. For that reason would always remain *the opium of the people.*"[41]

Based upon Feuerbach, Marxists seek a new solution in the social revolution of the proletariat. They insist that such a revolution ". . .will accomplish the radical surgery on the cancerous material conditions of modern society. When that cancer is removed, suffering will be eliminated, and the need for the opiate relief of religious illusion will be eliminated as well."[42]

Truly, today's religions appear weak, irresponsible, and senselessly caught up with the status quo in the midst of a miserable world. And, it is true that they make no solid proposals for curing these ills. Moreover, institutional religion focuses on its own maintenance and on keeping its hold on power. This is not so all for the religions, but the mainstream churches certainly seem to be preoccupied with these things at the expense of undertaking serious spiritual labors. Thus, today's religion is a target--and maybe a legitimate one. So people leave the church . . .

It is therefore important to know how materialism has affected the American church and society. America is driven by capitalism. Materialism is therefore one of the main threads running through everyday life here. This study therefore poses the following question: Is American materialism of the same type that Marx criticized?

One answer to this is to be found in the book, "The Spirit of America," edited by William J. Bennett. He begins by asking, " . . . what can we possibly learn about virtue from men and women of the eighteenth century? What could they possibly teach us moderns or even post-moderns?"[43] His questions suggest that America has been founded by great individuals and built on sound basic values–values that diverge considerably from those which underlie materialism. Bennett also insists that "We also need to restore this nation's sense of greatness, to learn once again about the great deeds and the great men and women of our past so that we might move forward."

What was the greatness of America in previous decades? Bennett first introduces patriotism and courage: "Patriotism means love of country, and it can call for great sacrifices and courage, perhaps even for the sacrifice of one's own life . . . It is our steadfast devotion to the ideals of freedom and equality. American patriotism, in short, is not based on tribe or family, but on principle, law, and liberty."[44] These legacies had been put into practice with the pen, not at the point of the sword.

Second, Americans seem to be centered on love and courtship, but as Bennett also notes, "For one cannot begin to talk about good citizens without consideration of the basic building block of citizenship—family . . . the love of a man and a woman is directed toward the raising of decent and honorable children—and good citizens."[45]

Third, civility is based in moral character and improves common life in so far as it emphasizes self-restraint and action with due regard to others. And also, friendship based on pleasure and utility does, as Aristotle notes, contribute to a better civil society.[46]

Fourth, Bennett emphasizes "education of the head and heart," based on the dicta "I can't tell a lie," "Know thyself," and "Be good." Every class of people should *know* and *love* the laws.[47]

Fifth, in its early decades, America focused on industry and frugality. People adhered to Benjamin Franklin's dictum: "Early to bed, and early to rise, makes a man healthy, wealthy, and wise . . . Ours is a country filled with men and women who began with little but a willingness to work and save and make good . . . . . . " John Locke also encouraged industriousness. He regarded it as a great virtue for democratic people given the benefits and the conveniences they enjoyed.[48]

Sixth, Bennett also focuses on justice as the goal of government and civil society. All men are created equal. "It ever has been, and ever will be pursued, until it be obtained, or until liberty be lost in the pursuit," said James Madison.[49]

Seventh, the American people believed the land is a blessing of Divine Providence. Indeed it was regarded as a new Israel in the eyes of many of the founders, e.g., George Washington and James Madison. Bennett concludes that "In America, unlike any other country of the time, the founders envisioned a land where people of all faiths could worship God without fear of persecution . . ."[50]

Thus, America was built upon on the spiritual values of love, courage, liberty, education, industry, civility, frugality, justice, law, piety, etc. It was not intended to be a materialistic and secular culture. Marx's materialism had effectively no place in nineteenth century American political and economic thinking. Still, we see what has developed now by way of a materialistic mindset in America. But, again, what exactly do we mean by this? What causes it to define everyday life for us?

American materialism can be described in three ways. First, scientific technology fosters America's move toward a materialistic society. Following upon the second wave, namely the development of industrial society, America is famous for being a technocratic society with its space science, aircraft, information culture, and sophisticated manufacturing processes, etc. Technological society gives priority to production of material goods, millions of identical products. As Alvin Toffler states, "On this technological base a host of industries sprang up to give Second Wave civilization its defining stamp . . . The new technology powered by the new energy system opened the door to mass production."[51] In particular, "We are entering the time when universal consciousness manifests itself through the Internet, an omnipresent oneness."[52] The development of the internet has brought great progress as far as our ability to remain connected with family and friends. It does mitigate against social isolation, loneliness, depression, etc.[53]

However, it also causes us to indulge our personal desires online. And, it encourages Americans to dream by encouraging them to purchase material things. In fact, Americans probably do not want to cut back on their spending on material goods given that the country is a consumer society. "Today's youth are too focused on buying and consuming things, and 58 percent describe most American children as *very materialistic*."[54] They are falling into a material lifestyle which makes it possible for them to be comfortable through easy and quick access to information and entertainment—ease of living at all any cost. But, this trend drives them away from genuine spiritual values and obstructs the process of soul searching. Marianne Williamson talks about a sinking feeling which she has when she sees America losing its spiritual force: "The principles underlying our social, political, and economic conditions deem us purely material rather than spiritual beings, economics rather than relationship-oriented, and separate bodies rather than united hearts."[55] In short, the value, worth, and spiritual strengths of our ancestors are being severely corroded–and maybe even replaced—by materialism.

American society is becoming materialistic because the technocracy stimulates the people to "Buy, buy America"—and it does so by manipulating people to yield to the every whim. They have to work hard and put in long hours in order to purchase material goods. This itself it makes for exhaustion and distraction from spiritual purpose – so people sleep in on Sunday instead of going to church. Technology increases materialism and consumption, both of which undermine spiritual discipline and values. People are becoming desensitized to these values and increasingly unaware of the legacy of their forbearers. Technology may help people lead a comfortable or even luxurious life, but it may be swallowing us up spiritually. It certainly does not move us to any further levels of spiritual awakening. In fact, it may be causing people to turn away from the divine. And, at present, people, seem to regard technology as king and material goods as God. The church is no longer a vital center of life.

Finally, I would like to ask whether the Christian church is itself materialistic or not? Is it above or beyond materialism? How does it relate to it? To answer this question, notice the many of the meetings that take place around the church community. Mostly the conversation at these meetings centers on management, on how to keep the church afloat financially. In the case of the mega churches, the collected monies are being utilized to invest in businesses and industrial products. Pastors and church leaders look like CEOs, and some of them are even involved in fraud and corruption. But, the institutional church is intended to provide jobs for pastor and bishop in the name of God, not to become preoccupied with money games and competition for promotions. Today, there are few ministry meetings on how to form disciples of Jesus and work for the transformation of the world. Today's church is not only a club house and a fellowship center, but struggling in the money game. It is not much different than a poor company which is going out of business. It looks like a divine institution, but it deals in material values rather than teaching and modeling spirit and social responsibility. That's how materialistic it has become. And, this is the way to kill the church. Life needs challenges and stimulation, we need to move toward newness and to continually re-awaken to spirit. But materialism is blocking this forward movement. Everything seems to cling to the status quo, including the church.

THE INSTITUTIONAL CHURCH AND THE STATUS QUO

Humans create religion and it is propagated by institutionalism. These are two sides of the same the coin. However, Jesus never had the intention to establish the church in his time. In fact, he had a seriously antagonistic relationship with the Jewish institutional temple. For this reason, he said, "I tell you the truth, the tax collectors and the prostitutes are entering the kingdom of God ahead of you." (Matt. 21: 31). Finally, he was crucified due to this conflict with Jewish institutional leaders.

Jesus' followers were eschatologically oriented life and felt much wonder in the face of life. They were awaiting the end of the world after their master's death, because they believed that Jesus' second coming would occur immediately. "They lived as those expecting the end of the world. The more they detached themselves from this world in their everyday actions, the more they kept destroying this world in their mystical fantasies . . ."[56] . And also, they were full of disappointment and fear in the face of their political opponents in this world. They expected it world would be destroyed, because it was full of the evil. Therefore, they did not seem to have any intention of establishing a worldly church.

However, the Gospel says that " . . . you are Peter, and on this rock I will build my church . . . " (Matt. 16; 18) –a verse that refers to the building the church by Jesus. Nevertheless, most modern New Testament theologians do not believe that these words were spoken by Jesus. Instead, they claim that they came from a later disciple. But, again, the "church" does not mean a building, but rather the people of God. This is why Peter was recognized and authorized as a divine leader by Jesus.

Even though Jesus was not interested in the establishment of the physical church, "sympathetic families were probably the nucleus of later local communities . . . It may have been the home community for the first Christian wandering charismatic."[57] Eventually this group was turned into the Christian community. "According to Luke, the earliest community in Jerusalem was governed by twelve apostles."[58] (Acts 1.12 ff). Thus, "the home community in Jerusalem endeavored to maintain a general oversight of the new churches. . .(they) were in full possession of God's Spirit, and (aimed) to encourage them in prayers and exhortation."[59] James, a brother Jesus, was the head of the church in Jerusalem. "With him were associated a council of elders, including the twelve companions of Jesus known as apostles.[60] The Christian church was then established by missionaries on a wider scale from village to city. M. Shepherd speaks about the expansion of the early church:

> The nucleus of membership of the new societies was gathered from the synagogues, where both Jew and Gentiles would already be familiar with the promise of God's Messiah and kingdom. Naturally most of the Jews were unconvinced that Jesus of Nazareth was the Christ (i.e., the Messiah). Accordingly, Christian believers were invariably expelled from the synagogues and forced to organize as independent churches. Of Paul's extensive missionary activities we are fortunate in having a fairly full record in his extant letters and in the Book of Acts . . . Paul was only one of man devoted pioneers in Christian evangelization.[61]

It was natural for the early Christian church to organize its own group to maintain peace and safety under the conditions of antagonism from the Jewish community. Even though it was organized as an independent church, the groups that constituted the early church were purely evangelical in purpose. Whatever they did, the early church had a message to be preached: "Jesus was died and risen for salvation and then ascended in heaven and coming back for the righteous judgment."

Bishops, elders, and deacons began to appear in the early church. "These are in a certain sense charismatic men. They have been made bishops by the Holy Spirit. But they are recipients of a charisma which makes them a definite group having particular duties to the congregation. . ."[62] This shows that the early church had already begun to institutionalize a hierarchical system of leadership. But, the organization had struggles within and among their leadership in the Philippic and Corinthian churches. Sectarianism was already becoming a chronic disease.

After the first Christian community was formed, the second era of the Christian community began. It was defined by dispute about dogma and extended from the middle of second century to the end of fourth century. Dogmatic issues escalated into confrontations among the early Christian fathers, the major leaders Clement and Origen and spread throughout communities of Jewish Ebionites, Alexandria, Antioch, and the Nicaean and Chalcedonian Creeds. *Homoousios* became a crucial issue: "the Son is out of the Father's substance and that He is of the same substance as the Father' and . . . not from any other *hypostasis* or *ousia* . . ."[63] On this dogmatic formulation, many people suffered and died due to the fact that they held opposing views.

In the process of its institutionalization, Christianity has seen tumultuous times where dogmatic and theological issues are concerned. Murder and war have also been a part of its history. The Crusades, a famous as a series of holy wars, were undertaken by militant Christians from the eleventh to the thirteenth centuries with the aim of recovering the Holy Land, Jerusalem, from the Muslims.

Nonetheless, Christianity also impacted Greco-Roman society. Shepherd tells of the public reputation of the early Christian community in the time of emperor. He describes early Christian life in community and social fellowship as follows.

> . . . there were innumerable clubs and guilds and trade associations which afforded a modicum of social fellowship and mutual aid under the sanction and patronage of sundry pagan deities. These were purely local organizations, whereas Christianity was a world-wide society. The credential of baptism gave a Christian immediate access to a circle of sympathetic friends in many community to which he might move where there was a Christian church. Hospitality to the stranger was a cardinal virtue of Christian teaching . . . The churches also acted as employment agencies for members out of a job and insured means of support to those unable to find work. Members enjoyed social equality regardless of their station in worldly affairs. Master and slave, citizen and subject, rich and poor shared a common table and, if personally qualified, were alike eligible for any office in the community . . . [64]

Thus, the early Christian community was given considerable credibility for a time and enjoyed the support of secular society. This trend helped stabilize the church as an institution both socio-politically and culturally. At approximately this same time, Constantine decisively helped move Christianity to the mainstream by lending it the support of his political regime. He believed that "the Christian God had assisted him in winning his battles for control of the Empire, and he therefore desired a continuance of whatever divine help the Christian religion might afford in maintaining the peace and welfare of his rule. The clergies were exempted from taxation . . . Moneys were given the Christians to build churches; in Rome several large public buildings were turned over to them for use as sanctuaries."[65]

This was a great help to Christianity when it was officially condoned by the political system of the day. A clear link was established between politics and religion. But it was also tragic in certain respects because further institutionalization degraded its authentic character and substance. In fact, this is when power struggles and troublesome group dynamics developed. The divine institution was confronting the world.

The institutionalization of the church becomes decisive with the development of the Roman Catholic Church and its accumulation of massive political power. "Roman political institutions were based on the cities, on which the surrounding country was dependent, and Christian organization followed the same rule. The country districts were dependent upon and were cared for by the city bishops and their appointees . . . the life and work of the bishop and his immediately associated clergy was largely regulated."[66] The Catholic bishop was not only a religious leader but also secular leader who ruled over the society conjointly with the politician. Jewish religious leaders had similarly controlled people socio-politically and religiously in the time of Jesus. But, with the decline of imperial power (Charlemagne), the papacy rapidly rose to independence. Two French church leaders, Ivo, bishop of Chartres, and Hugo of Fleury, writing between 1099 and 1106, had argued that church and state each had their rights of investiture, the one being spiritual, the other, worldly.[67]

The Roman institutional church grew rich and came to possess to 43% of the lands in the Roman era. Many bishops and members of the clergy possessed personal property even though they had taken vows of poverty. They became a powerful ruling class in the society. Indeed, the church was becoming a dominant social institution rather than the divine entity it had been intended to be. The Pope came to be viewed as having greater authority than the Bible and the church. He was regarded as on par with God. Power of politics had been substituted for the Kingdom of God. The more the church became institutionalized, the more it became secularized. Everything was in the Pope's hands. But this was a long ways from the original intent of Jesus' teachings, because, alas, the church was in human hands.

Walbert Buhlmann describes the Roman Catholic as the Second Church in his book, *The Coming of the Third Church*. He outlines the reasons why the institutional church was collapsed:

> ... The church as an institution is harshly criticized by enlightened Christians, while traditionalist Catholics support her not so much for her message and her religious mission as for her social and humanitarian activity on behalf of the sick, the poor and children. About 80% of Catholics in West Germany, France and Italy see this as the first duty of the church. There is a marked lack of interest in the church ... Catholic Action and the large scale church organizations, the pride of the church in some countries in the last decade, have largely collapsed ... [68]

The Second Church as a more purely human institution had turned to engaging in politics in the name of God. Its corruption became widespread and the behaviors of its clergy were sometimes grossly immoral. Therefore, the pagan and secular trends of the Renaissance offered the gravest challenge to the church.[69]

Martin Luther stood up to protest its corrupt practices and reform the corrupted Church. "Drastic religious changes were vaguely foretold by some anxious observers of conditions before Luther, but nobody could predict where the new forces would first appear."[70] He became a great champion of protest against the corrupt institutional church. The Reformation was a tough road for Luther and he made many enemies. The Emperor aimed to destroy him, and the Popes and bishops were overtly hostile to the Reformation.[71] He was heavily criticized as a betrayer, a pagan, a son of the hell, and even the devil himself by the Roman Catholic Church.

Luther's Protestant Reformation began with an ambitious challenge. "In 1517, Luther penned a document attacking the Catholic Church's corrupt practice of selling "indulgences" to absolve sin. His "Ninety-five Theses," which propounded two central beliefs—that the Bible is the central religious authority and that humans may reach salvation only by their faith and not by their deeds—would spark the Protestant Reformation."[72] His message of reform was "*Sola Fideo, Sola Biblio, Sola Gratio.*" And, as he stated, "Salvation comes only from God's grace, not a human work." Still, this is a controversial theme in theology. Modern theology rather says that salvation is a cooperative effort between God and human beings.

The new dawn had come. "On April 17, 1521 Luther appeared before the Diet of Worms in Germany. Refusing again to recant, Luther concluded his testimony with the defiant statement: "Here I stand. God help me. I can do no other." On May 25, the Holy Roman emperor Charles V signed an edict against Luther, ordering his writings to be burned. Luther hid in the town of Eisenach for the next year, where he began work on one of his major life projects, the translation of the New Testament into German, which took him 10 years to complete."[73]

In conclusion, the Roman Catholic Church as the Second Church focused on institutionalization as it assumed power above the Bible and the church. But Luther reformed the corrupted institution and restored the authentic word of God. In the process, he lost all kinds of his privileges with the Catholic Church. But, in retrospect it is clear that he stayed away from the wrong place–from the corrupt institution of the church. Luther freed the Bible and the church from the Pope's control. The impact of the Reformation was so great that it resulted in the development of Protestantism. But did Luther return the church to Jesus' Kingdom movement? Is the Protestant Church more properly aligned with Jesus' views than the Catholic Church was? Is the Protestant church on the right path from the point of view of Jesus' teachings. Does it understand and practice the authentic word of Jesus?

It is true that the modern Protestant was emancipated from institutionalized Catholicism by Martin Luther. But it itself has recreated the original problem. It has become heavily institutionalized and factionalized in various ways. If the Protestant church is chartered and organized, it is formed and governed by a bishop, a superintendent, and a pastor and its congregation will act in the name of Jesus. But, what do each of these do routinely?

First, they play politics within the church community. They are focused on the bishop's election and they define the outcome in terms of race and gender preference.

Second, they are concerned with appointments, with getting ahead and going on to Conferences, districts, and other churches. Some pastors are consistently appointed to three points-parishes in marginal areas. By contrast to this, Superintendents can be appointed to the best churches, as their desires dictate. And, they can define their own responsibilities.

Third, people seem to want to collect apportionments from the local churches and congregations. The church which collects the largest sums of money receives greater recognition than that which contributes a smaller portion.

Fourth, people are entirely focused on collecting, managing and administering money at the expense of supporting the ministry.

Fifth, they don't seem interested in discuss how to improve and revitalize the church in this period of decline.

Sixth, they don't talk about outreach program or seem interested in making people into disciples of Jesus, nor do they have the transformation of the world at heart.

Seventh, they don't discuss the quality of the leadership that is required of an authentic servant.

Eighth, they also don't take seriously Christian responsibilities in our miserable world. To the contrary, they basically ignore what is going on outside of their community. The connection between the church and the community has, for all practical purposes, been severed.

Ninth. The church is in crisis; it is in decline. But the pastor survives all the way. The Congregation becomes a stepping stone for the pastor to fly to the next door.

Tenth. The church praises the Lord on Sunday, but they worship Him as an idol. It doesn't talk about the authentic words of Jesus or envision and work for the Kingdom of God.

While church is somnolent and the worshippers are bored and disinterested, group meetings and social fellowships go on. Yet, again, there is an extreme and dangerous separation from the rest of the world.

The world is struggling with global warming, a massive flow of illegal immigrants, racial conflicts, regional wars, hunger and disease, etc. Currently, the USA is struggling facing the problem of illegal immigration, people sneaking into the nation. How to take care of them socially, politically and financially? Many parts of Palestine are being destroyed. How do we restore people's lives there? The minorities in Iraq are being exposed to the dangers of war once again and deadly situations are developing there in mountainous areas. Still, we don't hear any voices of concern from the American church. The poor, dispossessed and suffering people of the world are being cared for by governments and secular organizations rather than churches. Sometimes some of the church leaders try to speak out about these issues, but they are usually blamed by the congregations for being off message. The congregations themselves don't know that the Bible says about the world since they do not devote any time to study. That being the case, they are hardly in a position to respond to human misery and need. If this trend continues, the church will totally loses sight of its essential Biblical identity.

As a matter of fact, a church which does not concern itself with the world's issues may become spiritually and ethically emasculated. Trees which have no access to wind and water do not develop roots. In the absence of a genuine response to the challenges posed by the modern world, the church will only become weaker and weaker, then it will die. This is the way things are going with the institutional church. Their hymns lull the congregation in to a deep sleep. Furthermore, such stultifying conditions eventually enslave people, they dull their consciousness and disconnect them from world issues. But, again, this is the state of the institutional church today.

Thus, the institutional church was wandered far from Jesus' original teachings – and from his understanding of the need for atonement. Jesus represented for love and justice. These are at the core of the notion of the kingdom of God. He stood with the abandoned and the desperate in the midst of their suffering. His anger was directed against immorality and he stood up the socio-political power of institutionalized Judaism. The Jewish leaders had oppressed and exploited the people and Jesus' eloquent criticism was addressed to the traditional religious people who were obstructing the coming of the Kingdom of God. Finally, his life was consummated in death at the Cross. But, even in light of these facts, the modern church continues to transform itself into a job center, a club house, and a place for social gatherings. Jesus' would likely view it as a complete spiritual vacuum.

The early Church was born when the *kerygma* was proclaimed, the early Christian preaching about Jesus death and resurrection. According to Rudolf Bultmann, however, Jesus came into the world for the Kingdom of God. But His disciples praised the Lord as a Savior. They therefore lost the substance of the Kingdom movement and ceased to focus on righteousness. The second Church, Roman Catholic Church, developed as a sort of political power house which bore the name of Christ. However, it became corrupted by human desire. The Third Church, the Protestant Church, grew out of protested against the corrupt practices of the Roman Catholic Church. But it, too, has become institutionalized and stagnant as a result of merely following the status quo. The institutionalized Protestant Church seems not to want to labor to transform the world. To the contrary, it is unable to serve as an agent of change because of its own misguided and indifferent view of the Christian ministry. Indeed, the Protestant Church may finally have become a dead sect as John Wesley predicted–and it may be nearing the end of its time.

Chapter 2
THE CHURCH AS A STEPPING STONE

What is today's church? It is essentially an institutional church which operates under the aegis of church politics. Honestly, it is hard to describe it as Jesus' Kingdom movement and equally hard to attribute to it a genuine interest in fighting for righteousness in the midst of our miserable world. In the name of Christ, it attracts people who look for fellowship and jobs. And, as noted, it more clearly resembles a social and cultural center than a divine community.

It is true that many of the pastors view the church as a job opportunity. As soon as they are admitted as the members of Conference, they start to learn how to survive politically and even enhance their status there for life. They may improve their leadership skills with respect to the ministry, but they are equally likely to be concerned about how to become a bishop or a superintendent. They work hard at burnishing their reputation and image within the community for purposes of career development. And, when they find some reason to leave their church, the next one is conveniently waiting for them – a new appointment is just around the corner. The pastor always has an exit door and another door just about to open. But the church is being damaged by such behaviors. It should not be viewed merely as a stepping stone.

For a pastor, an appointment is a divine calling, an institutional commitment to carry out the mission of God. It is one way of following Jesus' command "Follow Me!" The Pastor surrenders herself or himself to Christ for the sake of the Kingdom of God and its righteousness, not in order to fulfill personal ambitions. God's will must always be supreme, "Thy will be done." This is how disciples are made and the world is transformed—and not in any other way.

However, these requirements are not taken seriously by today's pastors. They view their assignments merely as jobs and use them for further job seeking. Therefore, one can generalize that they have little genuine commitment to the ministry. Bishops and Superintendents earn high salaries as do government officials–they average $150,000 to $250,000 per year. Still, they do not make any significant difference for the church. And the Superintendent is given the privilege of choosing a still larger and more stable church when he or she is done the serving a term. The rich get richer and poor get poorer.

Some pastors attend seminaries and colleges for academic degrees such as an M.A. or a Ph. D., and they do this during the period of their appointments. Usually the three point church is a bridge for a pastor who wants to move to the next larger one. It is regarded as a place to practice or warm up for the next job, and so also a means to eventually ensure a sound retirement. Thus one is hard pressed to discern any sort of spiritual vision at most of the three point church; similarly for the larger ones.

When they obtain advanced degrees, they try to get teaching positions in the academic community rather than continue to work for the church. Clearly, the work of the church was not a priority for them, but only a means to an end.

There are a number of Korean churches in Madison. They have grown up over time and people are settled in the community. But the Korean United Methodist Church has unfortunately disappeared. (Currently it is being reinstated by the Conference.) It was financially supported by the Conference. So why has it vanished? First, the leadership failed where strategy is concerned also in its advisory capacity. Second, many of the pastors who were appointed to it were not committed to the church. Instead, they regarded it, too, as just a stepping stone, a bridge to something better. Therefore, they were not able to remain in the present and act in its true interest.

On the other hand, the growth of South Korean church is remarkable and has been documented over the course Christian history. American missionaries came to Korea in1884. Since they spread the Gospel there, six of the ten largest churches in the world are located there. In fact, a church can be seen on every street corner. But today's Korean church is getting a bad image in Korean society. They have money and lots of congregations. But the moral image is becoming tarnished. Moral hazards are many and they affect many pastors in this expanding church. The Roman Catholic was corrupted in the Middle Ages, too.

The Korean Protestant communities are the pastor-centered churches. The pastor is regarded as a sort of emperor and congregations are enslaved to him and serve the ministry blindly. The church has become capital-centered rather than Christ-centered. All of the growing churches are turning out business products for book stores, coffee-shops, restaurants, funeral homes, realtors, etc. The pastor has become a sort of CEO, he manages the business by sharing a portion of profits with the congregation. They are bound to together in a kind of symbiotic relation. If something goes wrong with the pastor where morality, sexually or finances are concerned, nobody blames him. This close relation makes it possible to conceal all such problems. And, such trends are also clearly at work in the American churches today, mega churches in particular. The reason why we see many of cases of fallen-ness in churches today is that the church has become money-centered. It is now very difficult to discern the Kingdom movement of Jesus and any Christian notion of true righteousness at work in such communities. And, the problem is now so extreme that the basic teachings of Jesus have even become obscured.

Furthermore, the Korean church is extremely hierarchical where the process of church election of staff is concerned. Many classes of people serve the church. There are the three types of lay leaders: elders, deacons, and stewards. The elder is a sort of first representative among the lay leaders. He is one of the main decision makers on the church council. He takes a royal seat in front of the public, and he has the power to contract or dismiss a pastor. But, he needs pay to the church anywhere from $10,000 to $30,000 to serve as an elder. This is big business for the church. The role of deacon is to visit and care for the congregation. He provides leadership at the small group bible study and prayer meetings. Finally, the steward serves, assists and visits the community. Whatever their position, these people have to pay something for the privilege of providing services to the church. There are volunteers pledge to serve in special positions. Supposedly, they are chosen for the greater glory of God, but, in fact, it is to serve their own desires. They are eager to enhance their social status and reputation, to put their titles on their business cards. Needless to say, morally and ethically this is questionable at best.

For these reason, the whole idea of a divine calling is being obscured in the church. It is rapidly fading from people's consciousness, a kind of mass moral amnesia seems to be setting in. And, without any anchor in the notion of a divine calling, the church is turning into merely a job-site for pastor. And, pastor may be alive, but the church is dead. Today's church retains the function of a social and cultural center and little else. If a pastor does not have a divine calling, he probably has a burning ambition to get ahead professionally and socially. And, he or she does not have any sort of divine calling, then a kind of rigor mortis has already set in.

WHERE IS THE CHURCH IN THE WORLD TODAY?

This section begins with the question, "Where is the Church in the World Today?" i.e., "What is it doing now?" My point here is to examine and critique the function of the modern church over against the historic facts and teachings relating to Jesus' life and death.

Today, we are facing a sort or tsunami of social change and social pressure. Ours is a radically changing society, one in which we are not able to predict what will happen tomorrow. So many issues are continually emerging which are in need of a moral and ethical response. Take for instance, the spread of drugs, the problem of student debt, the unavailability of health care, veterans' rights, youth unemployment, gun violence, illegal immigration, homosexual marriage, economic disparities, lack of moral leadership, terrorism, racism, police brutality, international conflicts and war, etc.

We need to pose some serious questions here. Do these issues not relate directly to today's church? And, is it not a part of the Christian community? Will we go on praising the Lord inside the church, enjoying the stained glass and the music, yet putting forth such a cacophony into the world where church politics are concerned? This is a quiet but burning issue.

Let us take a look at the authentic image of Jesus. He was born in a manger, in the lowliest of circumstances. Yet, he stood for the abandoned and the oppressed and the suffering in this world. He cried out for love and justice. He was savagely treated by the religious leaders of his day, and finally brutally murdered on the Cross. He is not a cement statue hanging on the Olympic stadium in Greece. Nor is he an idol which is worshipped by the people. Instead, He saved us from sin. He stood for divine righteousness in this broken world. But, does today's church stand for this? Do we see his spirit at work in our church communities today?

St. Paul said, "The church is the body of Christ." So, who and where is Jesus when we take communion? His disciples were invited to the table to continue teaching the Gospel, to carry out his instructions for teaching and living peacefully in the world. The breaking of bread symbolizes Jesus' sharing and surrendering his whole being to God for the sake of the salvation of the world. The spilling of wine from the cup symbolizes Jesus' giving his life for the world, without any constraints and in a spirit of atonement. Jesus was present in the world yesterday, He continues to be today, and will be tomorrow. So, where is such the Church today?

Let us ponder the theological role of the church as understood by Dietrich Bonhoeffer, a widely recognized theologian and pastor and well-known historic figure. He was introduced as a role model of faith for many Christians in the Methodist magazine, Good News, 2008. Bonhoeffer participated in the resistance against Adolf Hitler, and was executed by the Nazis in 1945, during the final months of World War II. On the way to his execution, he said to a prison guard, "This is the end, but for me it is beginning of life."[74]

Bonhoeffer wrote a theological discourse on freedom, responsibility, and obedience in confronting the world as a Christian. Dallas M. Roark explains his thinking as follows:

> To offend the conscience and to have responsibility, there must be freedom. The freedom that one has may seem questionable in light of environment, law, culture, routine, and other factors, but Bonhoeffer insists that freedom and responsibility prevail "in the encounter with other people." Freedom and responsibility are not isolated from but are related to obedience. In his words, "Obedience without freedom is slavery; freedom without obedience is arbitrary self-will. Obedience restrains freedom; and freedom ennobles obedience."[75]

Bonhoeffer addresses the triangular relationship of freedom, responsibility, and obedience where Christian ethics are concerned. These seem like three wheels of a bicycle. To develop a sense of obedience, the Christian needs to practice the commands of God in the world. Where freedom is concerned, he or she has to fight against oppression. And, as concerns responsibility, the Christian needs to be involved in the immoral world. The world cannot be a place of peace and love without the coordinated action of these three dimensions of ethical action.

When it does not acknowledge the need for obedience to the word of God, the church is prodigal and irresponsible. When it does not care for freedom, it is a slave to its own desires, and oppressed by them. Without a sense of moral responsibility, it is a tomb, merely a cement building. If it does not practice these, it is no different from a business or a social center. The true church, however, recognizes the need for all of these when it acts in the world on behalf of Christ.

Therefore, for the Christian, "Bonhoeffer now declares that a man takes up his position against the world in the world; the calling is the place at which the call of Christ is answered, the place at which a man lives responsibly. Vocation is responsibility and responsibility is a total response of the whole man to the whole of reality." The true Christian is in the midst of the world acting responsibly.

Bonhoeffer continues, declaring that "a pastor must be concerned for the whole church rather than merely for his own isolated flock. When a minister refused to raise his voice in the church struggle against the Nazis to defend other congregations or to protest persecutions outside his congregation, his own flock was eventually lost."[76] This is an excellent perspective for the modern pastor. He needs to embrace the whole world as congregation, to take care of business both inside the church and outside in the world.

The pastor's role is based on The Jesus' words: "I am the good shepherd; I know my sheep and my sheep know me . . . I have other sheep that are not of this sheep pen. I must bring them also . . . " (John 10: 14-16). Who are the other sheep outside of the pen? Some traditional church people belong in this category as do some secular individuals. This includes non-baptized and secular people, whoever is created in the image of God by has not yet been taken up into the fold. The whole world is the subject of Jesus' ministry. Therefore, church needs take care of it. Bonhoeffer was concerned with the world in the same was as Jesus was.

Furthermore, the Gospel of Luke introduces the Parable of the Lost Sheep. "Suppose one of you has a hundred sheep and loses one of them. Does he not leave the ninety-nine in the open country and go after the lost sheep until he finds it?" (Luke 15: 4). Jesus does not judge people based on material worth. Rather he focuses on intrinsic human value. This sermon aims at taking care of the sinner and not to the more than ninety-nine righteous persons do not need to repent. The ninety-nine sheep refers to the traditional religious people who are baptized under the traditional legalistic doctrine. Genuinely religious people are belong in such a category. Truly, they were not the priority for the Jesus' ministry. Instead, for Him, it is the sinners who are abandoned on the streets who are the subject of his Kingdom movement. Therefore, the church needs to turn to the world, even with all of its woes.

Today's church faces a vital question: Whom does it love? First, as noted above, it seems to love church insiders. Second, it loves these who support it financially. People who tithe are highly recognized. In the Korean church, they are regarded as first class citizens. And then, it loves people who support the pastor. They are welcomed as a loyal members of the Christian family. But, there is effectively no place for worldly people. The American church recognizes only insiders and does not seem to care for the outsiders, for people who are struggling in the world. They overlook the Lost Sheep altogether, forget to take account of those who are wandering and misguided.

All of the modern theologies stand for the worldly issues. Korean Minjung Theology emerged out of the context of political struggle under a militant regime from 1970s to 1980s. Its approach is "from context to text" and it considers that "context is ahead of text." Minjung Theology begins with human issues, not biblical scholarship.

One of its towering figures, Prof. Suh Namdong speaks to this as follows:

> . . . these are indeed theology in praxis or theology in the actual context. I firmly believe that theological activities do not end with the exposition of biblical texts on the salvation or liberation of man by God. In the Bible, the Exodus, the activities of the prophets, and the event of the Cross offer new insights, but these texts ought to be rediscovered and interpreted in the context of the human struggle for historical and political today . . . [77]

Thus, theology involves both the work of interpreting Christ's teachings and developing proper ethical solutions to human problems which it encounters in the world. Human struggle and even agony cannot be foreign to it. It is impossible for it to function in isolation from the world. Accordingly, theology itself can help the church to move into, and act within, the world. Bonhoeffer said that *Jesus stands for the other*. The church must as well. It has to find the Lost Sheep in the midst of the ninety-nine righteous persons. To address this point, I develop the concept of the "Talk Talk Meeting" and "Open Window Church" in Chapter 4.

Where Christian social responsibility is concerned, we need to recall two important two stories from the Gospel. The story of Good Samaritan helps the church to learn about who Jesus is. (Luke 10: 25-37). It is the only one from the Gospel of Luke that begins with a question on "Eternal life." It was the key subject of Jewish institutional church and continues to be so today. Jesus taught that salvation comes through loving action. This was how the victim of thievery in this story was saved. But, St. Paul focused on faith instead of loving action. This interpretation of His teachings may itself cause people to neglect them. It may also make Christians reluctant to focusing on love and justice. It is why Bultmann insists that the Christian church is only focused on ritual worship. If he is correct in his assessment, then the church has lost sight of the essence of Jesus' movement. And, St. Paul's preaching has driven the Christian people into a kind of prison of slavery and blindness. For this reason, if we have the spirit of Good Samaritan, we can help maintain this world in love and peace. Is today's church practicing this in the spirit of Christ in the midst of the troubled world? (see also Matt. 25: 31-46.)

SOCIO-IDEOLOGICAL ISSUES

Racism is an undeniably important issue in the church today. It is a dangerous force and could destroy the church. It is not only hatred between black and white, but between any combination of races. To insist on homogeneity rather than heterogeneity is to create isolation and division. Today racism is still a serious cause of a social conflict and even international wars. People of different races are not acceptable to the homogeneous and biased congregation. It can even happen that a pastors may be not welcome due to racial difference. Sometimes cross-cultural appointments are just not successful--unfortunately. This, too, is against the teaching of Jesus'. But, racism and discrimination happens in the church because does not take seriously the work of transforming itself into the Kingdom of God.

Homosexuality also and issues relating to it are also possible causes of division and factionalism within the church. In my experience as a pastor, one senior member of the congregation stopped attending church altogether over this issue. He was opposed the church's stance on homosexual marriage. Such the people say that it is a social evil and against the teachings of the Bible. They claim that if the church continues to support it, they will turn away from the church.

To conclude this second chapter, the current decline in the church is a fact of life in all of the denominations in America. Technology increases materialism in a society, and this does not help the people to embrace spiritual values. It is too easy to merely be a consumer. People are becoming desensitized with respect to spiritual values and their religious legacy. It is not only the case that technology makes for comfort, but it may actually cause us avoid necessary and important life challenges. There is no motive to seek spiritual awakening. Materialism may be anesthetizing people to mandate of Christ's teachings and alienating them from the notion of the Christian community as a divine institution.

Second, the church is becoming institutionalized and stagnant by merely following the status quo. It has lost sight of the true content of the Kingdom movement and of the Christian righteousness and no longer seeks to transform the world. The declining church follows the status quo rather than facing challenges, and the laziness of its leaders contributes to further decline. The institutional church of the mainline denominations is also not able to reform the church or the society, because they don't see clearly that this is their task. They are hardly leaders in transformation of the world because they, justifiably, the targets of reform movements and cannot focus on their essential tasks. In the end, Christianity may become just one more dead sect as Wesley predicted.

Third, one of the decisive causes of the decline in the church is to be found in its socio-political behaviors. American society has been stable and peaceful for a long time. We have not had to deal with war for many decades. With the exception of the Revolutionary War, the War of 1812 and the Civil War, it has always happened outside of the country. The first and only direct, large-scale attack on our soil was the incident of 9/11. For this reason, America is very stable and crisis is far from people's minds. Such a socio-political conditions have desensitized people to tragedy and struggle. Therefore, the spirit of the people is weak and not able to sustain true desires or to understand the importance of prayer in everyday life. This itself makes for a kind of collectively vanity and indifference within the church.

Fourth, as noted, the church has become segregated from the world. And, people are becoming ever more isolated from each other. The refuge mentality of the church has created, and continues to create, a deep gulf between it and world. *Jesus stands for the other.* But the church is far from being in contact with the world. And, there seems to be no way of bringing them together again. The world is not subject to the dictates of the church. The Bible may talk about the world, but the church does not. In, fact it seems to the church be almost a social evil. It sometimes seems that today, secularism is all pervasive, i.e., worldly people are defining the Kingdom of God and the notion of righteousness when this should be the task of the church. That's why Jesus said "Prostitutes and tax-collectors are coming into the Kingdom of God ahead of you." And it is also why He claimed that people were making a "den of thieves of house of God." (Mark 11: 17).

Finally, the divine calling seems to be being effaced from people's consciousness. And, absent a clear sense of this divine calling, the church is being reduced to a jobsite for the pastor and a social club for the membership. It is being degraded and turning away from the divine mandate. It may have already lost sight of the substance of the Kingdom of God and the task of transformation of the world.

NOTES

1. Richard B. Willke, *And Are We Yet Alive?* Nashville, TN. Abingdon Press. 1986.
2. Douglas W. Johnson & Alan K. Waltz, *Facts & Possibilities* Nashville, TN. Abingdon Press, 1987
3. Wilke. p. 11.
4. Ibid. p. 10.

5. Ibid. pp. 26-27.
6. Ibid. p. 27.
7. Reggie McNeal, *The Present Future*, San Francisco. John Wiley & Sons, Inc. 2003.
8. Ibid. p. 1.
9. Ibid. p. 9.
10. Ibid. p. 9.
11. Ibid. p. 10.
12. Ibid. p. 19.
13. John Flowers & Karen Vannoy, *10 Temptations of Church*. Nashville, TN. Abingdon Press, 2012. p. 2
14. Ibid. p. 3-4.
15. Ibid. p. 19.
16. Ibid. pp. 29-38.
17. Ibid. pp. 41-56.
18. Ibid. pp. 60-62.
19. Ibid. pp. 63-64.
20. Ibid. pp. 75-87.
21. Ibid. pp. 109-134.
22. John S. Dickerson. *The Great Evangelical Recession*. Grand Rapids, MI. Baker Book. 2013. pp. 21-22.
23. Ibid. pp. 37-61.
24. Ibid. p. 67.
25. Ibid. p. 94.
26. Ibid. p. 103.
27. Thom & Joani Schulz, *Why Nobody Wants To Go To Church Anymore.* Tyndale House Publ. Carol Stream, IL. 2013. p. 23-26.
28. Hatae Kim, *A Guide to Philosophy* (in Korean). Seoul. Jongnoseojuk, 1987. pp. 97-97. This is one of the best introductory philosophical texts used in colleges Korea.
29. *Marx & Engels On Historical Materialism*, ed. Lewis S. Feuer. NY, NY. Anchor Books, 1959. pp. 47-48.
30. Webster's Dictionary. Cleveland. Simon and Schuster, Inc. 1988. p. 834.
31. Hatae Kim. p. 107.
32. Wayne C. Stumme, "Marx's Thought: A Materialistic Understanding of History," in *Christians & The Many Faces of Marxism.* Minneapolis, MN. Augsburg Publ. 1984. p. 60.
33. Ibid. p. 61.
34. Ibid. pp. 61-62.
35. Karl Marx, *German Ideology*: Part 1, in Reader, pp. 172-73.
36. Ronald F. Thiemann, "Marx's Thought Critique of Religion," in *Christians & The Many Faces of Marxism.* p. 52.
37. Ibid. pp. 52-3.
38. Ibid. p. 54.
39. Daniel L. Pals, "Religion and Personality: Sigmund Freud," in *Eight Theories of Religion*. Oxford, UK. Oxford Univ. Press, 2006. p. 64.
40. Ibid. p. 64.
41. Ibid. pp. 54-55.
42. Ibid. p. 56.
43. William J. Bennett, *The Spirit of America*. NY, NY. Touchstone Publ. 1997. p. 18.
44. Ibid. pp. 25-26.
45. Ibid. pp. 101-102.
46. Ibid. pp. 145-148.
47. Ibid. p. 266.
48. Ibid. pp. 271-272.
49. Ibid. pp. 313-314.
50. Ibid. pp. 365-367.
51. Alvin Toffler, *The Third Wave*, Bantam Books, NY, NY. 1981. p. 20. Toffler categorizes the twenty centuries of our epoch into three waves: The first is marked by the agricultu-

ral revolution, the second, by the industrial revolution and the third by that of information technology.

52. Lance Secretan, "The Spirit of Work," in *Imagine*. Philadelphia: Global Renaissance Alliance. 2000. p. 132.

53. Dean Ornish, "Health," in *Imagine Magazine*. Cambridge, MA. No. 26, Sept 2005. p. 47.

54. Various internet resources and articles: "American Attitudes about Materialism, Consumption, and the Environment"; "Is American materialism increasing?" from *Materialism in America* (electronic journal).

55. Marianne Williamson, *Healing the Soul of America*. Simon & Schuster, NY, NY. 2000. p. 39.

56. Gerd Thiessen, *Sociology of Early Palestinian Christianity*, Trans. from German, Fortress Press, Philadelphia, PA.1978. pp.15-16.

57. Ibid. p. 17.

58. Ibid. p. 8.

59. Massey H. Shepherd, "The Rise of Christianity," in *A Short History of Christianity*, Ed., Archibald G. Baker. Chicago, IL. University of Chicago Press. 1940. p. 9.

60. Ibid. p. 10. See also the opening section of *Early Christianity*.

61. Ibid. pp. 10-11.

62. Williston Walker, *A History of the Christian Church*, Charles Scribner's. NY, NY. 1952, p. 52.

63. J. N. D. Kelly, *Early Christian Doctrines*, Harper & Row Publ., San Francisco, CA. 1960. For further details, see pp. 232-237.

64. Shepherd, pp. 25-26.

65. Ibid. p. 34.

66. Ibid. pp. 208-209.

67. Ibid. p. 233

68. Walbert Buhlmann, *The Coming of the Third Church*, St. Paul Publications, London, UK, 1976. p. 14.

69. Ibid. p. 98.

70. Ibid. p. 99.

71. John McNeill, See more detail, "Christianity in the Reformation Era," *in A History of Christianity*, pp. 99-134.

72. Various internet sources.

73. Various internet sources.

74. Dietrich Bonhoeffer, *Life Together*, Trans. John W. Doberstein. Harper & Row, San Francisco. 1954. p. 13.

75. Dallas M. Roark, *Dietrich Bonhoeffer*. Word Books, Waco, TX. 1972. p. 104.

76. Ibid. p. 105.

77. Suh Namdong, "Toward Theology of Han," in *Minjung Theology*. Orbis Books. NY, NY. 1981. pp. 57-58.

Chapter Three

Ten Reasons Why the Church Is Dying

1. Desensitization of why the church is dying
2. No seriousness of the church decline
3. Emasculation of leadership
4. Following status quo
5. Lack of calling to God.
6. Church is turning into a job center and cultural center
7. Church is stepping stone for the next door.
8. Church does not deal with the world issues
9. Church does not bring people
10. Church is segregated from the world.

Chapter Four

Some Opinions on the Solution of This Problem

In this chapter, experienced pastors and lay people talk about their opinions and make suggestions for coping with the problem of decline in the church. Their remarks express the reality of the situation and suggest solutions to it. They are not people who are merely sitting at the edges of the table of the community, but rather have been working in it for a long time. Church

leaders here outline a decisive direction for restoring it and freely exchange opinions and share ideas.

SOME LESSONS FROM EXPERIENCED PASTORS

Some Thoughts on the Decline of the Christian Denominations in America, By Pastor Donald E. Zelle, Retired Pastor, Lutheran Church, Beaver Dam, WI

Many major changes have taken place in America over the years. The population has shifted from 90% to 4% rural in the last hundred years and this has made for less stable communities. When communities are not stable, the same is the case with congregations. As people migrate from community to community, it is easier to leave the church behind and not re-connect with it elsewhere.

There has also been a shift in education. In the nation's early years, churches were the main providers of education, from elementary through college. People depended upon them and their related institutions for their education. At one point, the majority of the nation's congressman had theological degrees! However, the church no longer plays this role in American life and so people have less need for it.

There has also been a shift in the distribution of welfare resources. Again, early America saw the churches building and operating hospitals, nursing homes, children's homes, etc., institutions which were vital to many of American families. As government began to meet these needs, the churches became less involved.

And, there has also been a shift in the overall level of knowledgeability and an expansion of scientific knowledge. For many people, the Church no longer addresses or even agrees with modern science—to such a degree that Christianity has become relegated to the back burner in people's lives. Today's churches and their pastors must work hard to be deemed credible by intelligent people and to avoid causing cognitive dissonance lest they shy away. Any old fashioned views and/or overly literal interpretations of the Bible which are lacking in serious scholarship of its origin give cause for skepticism. Pastors have to build a new level of discipline into their weekly routine of preparation for preaching and teaching.

In many arenas of American life, the Church has become the caboose of the train rather than its engine. Society often makes corrections and adaptations long before the Church does. Voting rights for women are a case in point. At church, they sat across the aisle from the "men's side"), or took their proper place. There is also the issue of slavery and race relations. Where were the early Martin Luther Kings of the Church? Where are they now? We ought also to consider the currently debated issue of homosexuality. And, what about responsible sex and birth control and the use and abuse of the prison system? Where is the Church in respect to local and community leadership? What about local, state and federal government? It tends to speak only when someone else has raised a social or moral issue, but, in fact, it needs to be the engine for positive social change.

The record of the clashes of denominations does not reflect a huge influx of members. Doctrinal disagreements need not lead to divisiveness. Creedal statements and old church liturgies need to give way to meaningful expressions of faith for the majority, not the minority. We need a more broad-minded Church, one that accepts a variety of responses to the revelation of God in Jesus Christ.

There has been a change in the role played by pastors. Where they once taught weekdays in the church schools or were guests at the homes of church members and advisors in the local communities, where they made contacts with new citizens, were always present to provide spiritual care and basically servants of the community, now many have stepped back into their own worlds where professionalism is the order of the day and meetings, seminars and Sunday worship consume all of their time. Preaching has become more topical than biblical. As one pastor said, "I don't make calls on people to invite them to worship. I expect the word to get out and they will come, and once here they will return." Another said, "My weakest attribute is that I am uncomfortable making "cold calls," or "evangelism calls." Such pastors find it easy to dress in attire that makes it appear as though they are on vacation and they do not expect to be in contact with members of the congregation or the community until they are present at Sunday worship.

In relation to the above, denominations of the Church have become too institutional, too protective of the status quo, too hierarchically minded, and they now spend too much energy on maintaining the system.

There are, however, exceptions to all of the above. This writer is fortunate to belong to a congregation that is vibrant and has top notch worship services with a great variety of music. Its outreach does put them in contact with Main Street and it provides weekly meals for all and health services for those in need. It also maintains a schedule of seasonal observances for the community and sends people out to help others throughout the nation and the world. There are many adult learning opportunities in the community and a thriving Sunday school. And, it co-operates with other congregations on a variety of levels.

In some parts of the world, the Church is involved in almost every aspect of people's lives. Their churches therefore are vibrant and even expanding and their worship is filled with joy. The Church gives them cause for hope makes them resourceful. Would that the Church in America and its many denominations and congregation could catch a glimpse of what a Church can be. It might them be able to transform itself into to a beacon of hope for the people.

How to Face the Problem of Decline in the Local Church, By Scott Carlson, Superintendent UMC, Wisconsin

During my time as a career pastor, I have always been concerned about the decline that is taking place in the mainline churches of North America. On an average weekend, more people stay away from worship services than come to them. This is a development that has occurred during my lifetime and my career and I truly lament it.

While I think there are many ways we can face and combat this decline, I have sought to face it down by working to help the church I serve (currently Sun Prairie United Methodist Church, in Sun Prairie, Wisconsin) to become a more healthy community.

If I am going to do this, however, the *first step has to be to understand who I am and how can I be a morally healthy leader*. Being a healthy leader means that I must work at taking care of myself physically as well as spiritually. I am committed to regular exercise and regular prayer.

Over the years, the time I allot to prayer has taken many different forms. I have even used different methods (see www.sunprairieumc.org/worship/methodsforprayer), but feature of many of them is to plan time for reading and reflecting upon scripture, quiet time for in which I can bring my hopes, dreams, concerns and fears before God; also, I schedule time for journaling and reflecting upon what I am hearing.

One of the main images I have for myself as a pastor, is that I am a player-coach, a coach in that it is my job as a pastoral leader to see the big picture and to encourage the congregation to listen to God's call as to where we need to go. Once that direction has been discerned, then it is up to me as a coach to help lead us there. Yet I am also a player who works with members of the church, side-by-side in ministry as we move forward together.

I have been heavily influenced by the writings and teachings of Edwin Friedman as he applies Family Systems thinking to organizations like the church. He has challenged me to understand that leadership is about being self-defined in a way that confirms me in my role as a leader, but, at the same time, ensures that I remain connected to the people I am serving.

There are several ways in which I stay connected to the membership of the church. I have intentionally blocked out times for conversation with the congregation, with the staff and the lay leadership. These conversations help us work together and take the steps that are necessary to for the church community to become healthy.

In the course of my career, I have done this in a number of ways. When I meet a congregation for the first time, I invite the entire congregation to one of many small group gatherings in the homes of different members of the church. During that meeting, we go around the room and make introductions and talk about the length of time in which people have been members of the church. Then we take time to visit about three questions (I have them write the answers on a half sheet of paper first): (1) What do you love about our church? (2) What do you believe God is calling our church to do? Or, what do you think our church will look like in twenty years if it is a healthy vibrant congregation? (3) What are you willing to do to help us go where God is calling us to go? Then at the end the discussion, I promise to tell people about myself and what is important to me.

Hearing people respond to these questions in the first several months at a new church not only allows me to get to know people, but it also gives me a very good feel for the strengths of the church. And, it helps me to understand their hopes and dreams for it. It also sends a signal to them that I don't want to merely do church as usual. If we are move into the future, to follow god's call, we have to do it together. Each member of the church needs to respond to God's call in their own life.

In addition, I allot regular times for listening to church leaders (committee chair persons) by inviting them to a team breakfast. I also plan intentional listening sessions with the congregation at large. Although I have not personally had formal supervisory sessions with the staff I work with, I regularly touch base with them about what is happening in their area of the ministry area and about their goals for their work.

A second step for trying to help the church to be healthy is to focus on, and stay focused on, our mission. Over the course of twenty-five years in the ministry, I have come to realize that churches either function out of a sense of mission or they cave in to the personal preferences of the leadership. It is always the most healthy to focus on mission and to get the congregation to look beyond the walls of their church and see the world and the people around them.

In the congregation I serve, I usually preach on our mission statement at least once a year. In addition, in our new monthly member orientation class, we focus on the church's role in helping people to connect with God and grow in faith. In addition, I have challenged our church so that each group that meets, be it a committee, a small group, a Sunday school group or a choir, is involved in one mission project per year. It is my hope that each week of the year we will have someone or a group of people somewhere in the world working on a mission project.

As pastors, we play a key role in ensuring the health of our congregations. This begins with our taking care of ourselves. We need maximal spiritual health. It continues with our helping our congregation stay focused on the mission of the church and on moving beyond the church's walls so as to meet the needs of the community in which we live.

In my opinion, the time in which we are living is one of the most difficult where a call to ministry in the Christian church is concerned. Yet, I have come to believe it is also one of the most exciting times ever in which we can say "Yes!" to God and give ourselves to the task of leadership. At this point in history, being a follower of Jesus Christ really does matter. It can makes a difference in many ways.

I want to be involved in helping people develop the most important relationship of all, namely, that with Jesus Christ. It is this relationship that helps them get out of bed in the morning and make sense of their world —when things in our world often do not add up at all! If we can have this sort of attitude, the best days of the church may still be before us.

Rev. Jim Cotter, Columbus UMC

As concerns, the qualities of a good pastor, my thinking is as follows:

- The ability to live with ambiguity. Pastors who see everything in stark terms may do well at communicating doctrine, but they fall short in managing human relationships.
- Listen and search for values. Listening is so very important. It does not involve merely hearing and absorbing information, but also interpreting what is conveyed. What are the values that are being shared?
- Read the Bible and think on how it educates us on the conduct of human relationships. It is our primary text, our spiritual anchor. It can be read literally, as a source of truth, or consulted as a guide in everyday life, as a source of life itself. I far prefer to read it as the latter. Jesus came that we might have life and have it abundantly. The Bible gives us many clues as to how to together on this planet, and how to be faithful to God.
- Find the courage to speak the truth in a spirit of Christian love. At funerals, we need to do two things: praise God and speak the truth. We need to talk about a person's life honestly and kindly. This is the approach that should always be taken. When we have a problem with someone, we need to address it is a spirit of truth and Christian love. This doesn't always go well, but God also doesn't guarantee outcomes. We just need to be faithful to Him—and when we are, we usually learn something in the process.

Circuit Ministry as a Turnaround Strategy for the Church, By Don Greer, Coordinator of Circuit Ministries, UMC, Wisconsin

The Circuit Ministry was established in the Wisconsin Conference of the United Methodist Church in 2003 as a way of organizing churches and clergy so as to ensure collaboration among them. The desired outcomes of this collaboration were identified as "new ministries with new people" and "finding things we can do together that we cannot do alone or as individual congregations." The plan relied on clergy circuit leaders taking the initiative at the local level to discover new things to do and organize group projects. They were also expected to fulfill a variety of administrative tasks related to the work of district superintendents because the appointive cabinet had been downsized by half (only four district superintendents had been assigned to a total of eight districts). The clergy circuit meetings were also intended to provide the first level of supervision and support for clergy. This made clergy circuit leaders accountable for the liaisons between district superintendents and pastors. Circuits had developed in a variety of ways without consistency or common points of focus. In 2012, a newly appointed coordinator for circuit ministry conducted in-depth research on the status of the circuits and the capacity for their redevelopment. The result was a plan to relaunch the Circuit Ministry with clearer focus on outcomes and well-defined processes; it also sought to ascertain what had previously worked and what not and to put into place appropriate corrective measures. At the core of this new thinking was a conference vision statement that had been developed by a new bishop in the first several months of his assignment in Wisconsin. The vision was entitled *Imagining Wisconsin Anew*. It aimed to provide the direction for a turnaround movement in the United Methodist Church in Wisconsin. It is described on the conference website as follows:

> *Imagining Wisconsin Anew* is an effort to bear good fruit by serving new people, diverse people, young people, elderly people, all people. The Wisconsin cultural and demographic landscape is changing, so United Methodists need to pay careful attention to the culture changes where there are United Methodist congregations. We are called to invest in new communities around the Conference waiting for ministry to be offered; and provide direction and forming productive responses, rather than simply reacting to changes. *Imagining Wisconsin Anew* means looking at who Wisconsin United Methodists are, the choices we can make, and the opportunities for transformation and vital witness.

The five areas of focus for *Imagining Wisconsin Anew* are: encountering multi-cultural communities, planting the seeds of new ministries, engaging the turnaround movement through the work of vital congregations, imagining ministries of mercy and justice, and imagining soul food in Wisconsin. The central concern for Circuit Ministry became how to reframe and reorganize the work of circuits in order to ensure these outcomes.

The relaunch of the Circuit Ministry made it clear that circuits are to be ministry producing units and not merely self-serving and self-perpetuating administrative structures. The practice of using Circuits for administrative functions attached to the Cabinet was therefore ended, as was that of using the appointed clergy circuit leader to perform proxy district superintendent functions. The intent in this was to reverse a pattern of burdening circuits with information or agendas for conference programs and instead allowing them to become effective, local research teams and think tanks which were creatively looking for ways to accomplish the goals of *Imagining Wisconsin Anew*.

One of the findings of this research was that clergy-driven circuits were ineffective in establishing a lasting vision for new ministry, largely due to the fact that the groups were almost always in a state of transition. It had proved challenging for the clergy to define a vision for the longer-term and the future because they were destabilized by itinerancy. Those few circuits that enjoyed continuity of vision and follow through in the practice of the ministry were the ones that had developed strong and effective lay leadership and a lay circuit group. Among these were groups that were not focused on program implementation alone, or event planning; instead, they were involved with strategic visioning and were cooperating with their clergy as strong partners. However, clergy driven circuits which attempted to get the laity involved in activities typically planned events and then attempted to get laity from their congregations to attend them or assist in the implementation. This approach resulted in only spotty success, and when it was successful it could seldom be replicated. For the most part, it resulted in ministries of shared nurture rather than new outreach ministries that were oriented toward new people. The strategy of relaunching the Circuit Ministry noted the experience of the circuits involving laity in strategic leadership roles. The new model therefore established a two part circuit including a Circuit Clergy Team and a Circuit Laity Team. They were assigned related, mutually complementary, but different, functions.

The function of the Laity Circuit Team was to study the region and imagine new ways to reach new people based on demographics, changes in population, new people they discovered to be resident in communities, and also on a working knowledge of the strengths and limitations of existing ministries in the circuit. As a think tank, they were tasked with generating new ideas, and identifying new possibilities for new ministries. They were to be trained to understand congregations as discipleship systems so that their thinking about new ministry options might be properly directed and their ideas might be brought to bear on the conditions in their own congregations. They were also to be trained in strategies for community research and social engagement, both of which would guide their creative work.

The Laity Circuit Team, together with the Clergy Circuit Team, would explore options for design and implementation of their new ideas (what would it take?) with the intention of then embedding them into existing United Methodist congregations, or developing collaborative strategies for churches within the circuit. New ministries would be connected to existing congregations if and when there was willingness and capacity. Rather than implementing any new ministry in a given congregation completely independently of others, there would be a hand-off. Congregations that accepted a ministry idea would plan, implement, experiment, adjust or adapt to make it their own. Meanwhile, the Laity Circuit Team moved on to work on still more new ideas. This approach is a sort of revitalization strategy for local congregations, one that works through collaborative research focused externally. The vision would come from the outside into the local church, rather than the more typical modus operandi, namely, from the inside out. And, specialized, selected laity and clergy would collaborate in a process of visioning the future. Rather than thinking about how to get more people in a community to connect to a church that is struggling with its own need for growth, this approach brings the needs of a community to the congregation.

The Laity Circuit Team, Clergy Circuit Team, and Local Congregation share three critical aspects of leadership:

- Visioning (Strategic Thinking)
- Futuring (Strategic Planning)
- Managing (Tactical Planning)

Although individual congregations incorporate all three elements in their own leadership and ministry, for Circuit Ministry 2.0 the specialized function of lay Circuit teams and clergy Circuit teams can be illustrated using three overlapping circles (see below). The lay Circuit team is associated with *visioning*, while the clergy Circuit team is more focused on *futuring*, and local congregations, both individually and collaboratively, are associated with managing or tactical planning. If the clergy and lay leadership of a local church possessed a degree of clarity about its own vision, they could inform others on the questions of fitness or viability of their community when the Clergy Circuit Team and Laity Circuit Team met to discuss possible development strategies for new ministries. Such conversations involve an overlap between what I have here termed *visioning* and *futuring*.

The new approach to Circuits would not be the same as the first one. Circuits would not be intended to implement program ministry in which all of the churches would be expected to participate. Instead it posed the question, "What is in it for the local church?" The answer is a visioning process that can see beyond the communally defined boundaries of the local church, and a process for discovering their next mission, should they choose to accept it. The plan also provides a framework for maintaining the longer-term vision for the church as a whole in a defined geographic area. It ensures that this plan and its implementation are not solely dependent on clergy who may be relocated. The process invites churches and clergy into new modes of collaborative ministry, but, at the same time, it does not diminish the importance of local congregations as the vital and central to mission and ministry.

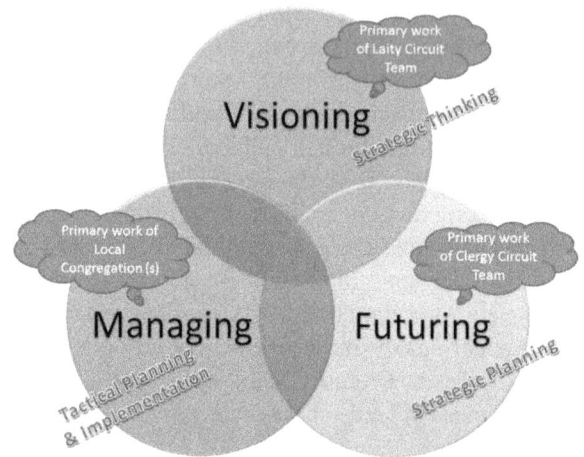

It is process, not program. It aims at long-term development and transformation, and so it not merely a quick fix strategy.

THE URGENT VOICES OF LAY PEOPLE

Some Thoughts on Why There Is Decline in Attendance at United Methodist Churches, By Verna Lambrecht, Gillett UMC

The Annual Conference seems to have forgotten that large churches came to be and grew due to the support they received from small rural churches. Today, it seems that the emphasis is on bigger, whether or not that is better. The Annual Conference is now held in large Conference Centers in major cities. This has resulted in higher costs to small rural churches when they cannot afford them. They therefore often have no representation where voting on future programs and the direction of the Church as a whole are concerned. And, when the small church reaches out to the Conference for help in growth for their Church, the ideas and suggestions they receive are generally geared toward cities rather than small communities.

Congregants get the feeling they do not matter, and, little by little, as small churches are closed those members either connect with other neighboring denominations or they fall away from the church altogether.

When a new Pastor who is assigned to the Conference, it often does no follow-up to see if the collaborative arrangement is working, nor does it give the Pastor the tools needed make it work. Nor does it check with the pastor to see if the congregation is helping to fill the gaps where the pastor may be lacking in skills.

Serving the Church of God is a team effort! Pastor and Congregation need to cooperate. Our Seminaries need to keep this in mind when they training individuals who are called to the Ministry. No Pastor should be expected to do it all, nor should he or she somehow be trained to do as little as possible.

What all of us need to keep in mind is that the ministry is not about either the pastor or the congregation. It is, first and foremost, about God and those around us that do not know Him.

The training of a Pastor should emphasize pleasing Him who called him or her to Ministry. One can never please an entire congregation, but if they are pleasing God, He will take care of the rest.

A Pastor needs to take an active part in the community in which his church is located. He or she needs to take an interest in those church members who are inactive, homebound or in nursing facilities. They are still members of the congregation and should be treated in the same way as those who attend weekly services.

In my opinion, there are two reasons for the decline in church membership: the ministers and the church conference.

Carol Swim, Tabor UMC

As I sit in church on a Sunday morning and look around, what do I see? Mostly, or entirely, elderly people. No one representing the younger generation! Why? Because church is boring. With an aging congregation, things seem to continue in the same old way. Sunday after Sunday, the elderly are satisfied with this, but the church has nothing to offer the young people, nothing to keep them interested. This problem can be traced back to the church leadership, the pastor or shepherd of the flock. People come into the ministry unprepared, or they are put in churches that are wrong for their personality, then these difficulties are reported back to the conference. Today's church is a business and not a religion. What has happened to the clergy who were genuinely committed to working with people to make changes and help motivate them to do more in their church? Where are they?

In my experience, today's clergy just seem to give sermons on Sundays, attend a few meetings and maybe visit someone in the hospital occasionally—and that's it. What are they taught in seminary? Are they taught to perform only these basic functions? Are they led to believe that the ministry is just a job like other run-of-the-mill jobs?

But, I would argue that the conference also contributes to this. Some clergy are placed in the wrong settings and sometimes certain churches are yoked together when conditions are not geographically right. When two churches are 30 to 40 miles apart, it is hard to do a decent job with either one. One gets all the attention and the other just drifts along.

So what is the answer to this problem? I confess that I don't know. Changes have to be made all around. The Conference has to spend more time and give more thought to placing clergy properly, and clergy have to be more prepared to handle all the situations that can come up in a church setting.

What You Should Expect from a Pastor,
By LoAnn Elbe Retired Teacher, Suring WI

1. Personal contact. He or she should get to know families, become familiar with names of the individuals and some of their likes and dislikes. Too many pastors do not actually know who makes up their congregation..
2. Pastors need to be available for funerals, weddings, baptisms. They have a schedule that they set and the people are expected to choose the dates for their events in keeping with that schedule. Some pastors now demand a fee for these services. They set their price and expect to be paid that amount. Sometimes, I think, the church could encourage individuals to become members if they occasionally performed one of these services gratis.
3. A pastor needs to be a leader in three areas: Spirituality, fellowship, and biblical scholarship. Today's pastors are more concerned to be present on Sunday rather than to be involved in the daily and weekly tasks which need to be done with and for the church community.
4. A pastor should stay true to the teachings of the Bible, its principles and truths. He or she should not merely deliver the messages to please a certain few in the church.
5. He or she should also make him/herself visible in the church and the community. This means becoming involved in activities and community organizations.
6. He or she should also organize outreach programs that will be available not only to church members, but also to others in the community.
7. A pastor should reach out in the community for new or potential church members.
8. Lastly, he or she should make the church a welcoming place, not just on Sunday, but every day of the week.

The Church: Surviving/Thriving in a Changing World,
By Susan Bentz, Moraine Park College Librarian, WI

I often imagine the church today as being persecuted as it was years ago when Christians were fed to the lions, i.e., in the time of Caligula or Nero.

Society that makes fun of professions of faith and so the faithful keep their mouths shut when they would rather be speaking out. They are afraid of ridicule from those who think church is for sissies and wimps. And, the media often belittles Christianity and religion in general. We have elevated ourselves to the rank of masters of the universe and see no need for a divine creator or redeemer—a form of arrogance which, as my pastor noted, is the essence of original sin.

Moreover, some churches just add to this religious foolery nowadays by being a front for money loving, smooth talkers who have learned how to manipulate the word of God. Others shun society altogether and keep hoping to avoid all worldly temptation. And, some churches tell their congregations how and what to believe. They encourage conformity instead of confrontation with difficulties, and so actually limit personal spiritual growth.

There is no doubt that the church has had difficulty keeping up with the changes in our society and culture. The ways of the world are often in conflict with the ways of God. We forget that the church has to meet sinners where they are, and not expect them to seek it out. Moreover, we need to be passionate about the people Christ was passionate about—the hungry, the poor, the sick, the drug addicts and the prostitutes. Worship happens inside the sanctuary but our ministry and service begin as we leave the church and enter the homes, offices, factories, streets and buildings that comprise our community, where we actually meet the people of God's world. This is where our faith is put to the test, refined and strengthened.

If the church is to survive, we must realize that faith is a matter of an individual relationship and a journey to God, a journey that each one of us takes within the real world. The Father put us in this world where we live out our faith relationship with Him. But we are not *of* this world. Through our faith relationship we belong to God. Still, our faith is to be lived out daily in this very real, and sometimes very gritty and troubled, world. This means that we need to question the path on which we are traveling, and ask God to give us direction in our lives.

The church also needs to be a vital part of the community, living organism that enhances its well-being and keeps it properly centered in spiritual values. It needs to welcome sinners and freely forgive them. And, Christians need to strengthen each other through the practice of brotherly love, and encourage each other to work through questions and difficulties in order to grow in their faith. And, sometimes this requires real struggle, facing the tension between our own free will and God's will for us. In difficult times, in particular, Christians need to provide each other encouragement and strength.

God does not abandon us when we question him. He wants us to know him fully and He will reveal His plan to us if we just allow this to happen (Jeremiah 29:11). Sometimes all we have to do is listen in silence; other times we need to act.

Our clergy must also be part of the real world. They must experience the ups and downs of daily life just as everyone else does. However, it is not ultimately their responsibility to save the church. We, both clergy and laity, are the church, the one body, and it will take all of us to revitalize it. Living one's faith through witness and discipleship in today's world is not for the faint of heart. Sometimes we may be made fun of or ridiculed, but Christ compels us through His Word and reminds our Christian brothers and sisters to share the good news, keep the faith and persevere. We pray, 'Thy will be done,' and when we are truly willing to follow God's lead, amazing things will happen.

Prof. Ruth Lindergarde, Lowell UMC, Wisconsin

Calling upon members of congregations will build church infrastructure. It will helping them support people who have chosen to go into the ministry, and/or who are doing missionary and community work. It is the task of the church leadership to support our youth and ensure their future well-being. We can draw on the theology of abundance to do this, even though it runs directly counter to the current trend of decline in the church. Moreover, this will successfully build the connections necessary for creating and nurturing an environment in which people can hear God's call. Consider Isaiah 6:8: "Whom shall I send, and who will go for us? Then said I, Here am I; send me."

The work we do every day is not ultimately meant to benefit ourselves only. It is rather done for the common good, for everyone in the world. No matter what type of work it is, from caring for your children or running a business at home, to serving at an organization in any professional or volunteer capacity, work always plays a vital role in making the world a better place. God makes use of everyone's contributions in his ongoing effort to save us from our fallen-ness. Reminding yourself of this will motivate you to do your best work any setting. In the process, God will weave your work into his own so that it can have a real effect on the world around you.

How can churches call churches? Congregations need to be welcoming and to encourage young people to dedicate their lives to Christ. Sunday school, Vacation Bible School and youth groups are one avenue of approach to this. Church members need to support young people by asking them what difference they want to make in the world. What do they want to do? Are there things they like to do? Congregational members can do this and Sunday school teachers need to recognize the importance of the leadership role they play. It can help students to dedicate their life to Christ not only in a religious context, but also in their work and community settings. Congregations are capable of noticing emerging leadership skills and encouraging their development in young people for the greater glory of God. Congregations who experience and encourage these callings have an overall sense of vocation and generally good relationships with their young people. This can seem like a difficult task, but members need to share their faith with the young. Doing so amounts to supporting to them in their faith and has a lasting and positive impact on the world around us. Members of congregations need to understand and share their sense of calling. In his writings to the church in Corinth Paul uses the language of vocation (1 Corinthians 1: 2-26 and 1 Corinthians 7:17-24).

A *greenhouse of hope* is a Christian congregation which supports its members with traditional ways of following Jesus. They respond to God's love through practices that genuinely embrace the gifts of youth and young adults. From these greenhouses there then emerge young leaders who do want to change the world.

Leadership in the Christian Community: It is important that churches have transitional leaders in the church and congregation. Members of the congregation need to be thinking about talented individuals who can take on leadership roles in the future. Leadership cannot be taken for granted. Young people need to be challenged to understand their call to leadership in the church. Members of the congregation need to nurture and support the youth if they are to eventually take on these roles. The call to leadership is in some respect intentional, but so is the work of developing one's skills. Pastors need to create a space for the laity for this and also to find opportunities to lead with their own skills.

True leaders are humble, purposeful and prayerful because they have a commitment to honor the will of God. Leaders work as a team and develop the talents of other leaders by sharing their good and bad experiences with them. A church leader shares information with others and does not withhold it, particularly when it is useful for the growth and development of the church. There are no perfect leaders but a leader is above average in character. Unfortunately, there is always someone who will is critical of the leadership. Leaders therefore need to continually prove that there are trustworthy. A good leader uses his/her influence for the benefit of others and not for his or her own material gain.

Leaders also have skills that support the church. Their sense of professionalism helps them ensure that things are done in the best way possible. Good leaders support others' efforts to become great leaders and are not threatened by anyone else's success. They are focused on serving their church and love and value others. Successful leaders are also dedicated to continual and new learning and to implementing what they have learned into the church. They are accessible, approachable and accountable for their actions as they are aimed at the betterment of the church. Leaders are visionary, and their vision centers on the future of the church and the well-being of its members. Lastly, they have integrity and are driven by an overriding commitment to spirituality.

Each congregation needs to put together a plan for supporting young people and nurturing their capacities for Christian Leadership. The youth of the church need to be empowered to stay in the church and they need to feel that they can become leaders—not left in isolation from adults to merely find their own way in what is now becoming a very difficult world.

LEARNING LEADERSHIP FROM THE BUSINESS WORLD

Today's church members need to look through their windows, so connect with the world around them. What is going on in the business world? There things happen in revolutions, waves, and tempests. Yesterday, an establishment was on the street corner, but today it is gone with wind.

Futurist scholar, Alvin Toffler, predicted that there would be waves of revolutions and that they would take shape in various ways. In his view, they would affect every corner of our life as follows:

> He believed that the coming civilization would be so profoundly revolutionary that it would challenge all our old assumptions. Old ways of thinking, old formulas, dogmas, and ideologies, no matter how cherished or how useful they were in the past, would no longer fit the facts. And, indeed, the world that we are seeing emerge from the current clash of new and old values and technologies, geopolitical relationships, lifestyles and modes of communication, demands that we adopt entirely new ideas, frame new analogies, and work out new concepts and systems of classification. We cannot cram the embryonic world of tomorrow into yesterday's conventional cubbyholes! Nor are orthodox attitudes or moods appropriate.[1]

This is a wholesale revolution turned upside down. If we cling to our old ways of thinking, the ground could soon collapse from under our feet. This new wave of challenges— which sometime takes on the proportions of a tsunami—provides the backdrop for our working out a new paradigm for our survival. Indeed, we are compelled to do this while the world trembles! [2]

Since we have experienced three way revolutions: *time, space, and knowledge*, every day brings rapid changes on many levels and in many areas of life. Yesterday's theories are today's refuse, yesterday's textbooks are now useless heaps of paper. And, this sort of thing is happening every day in our lives and in the business world.

The Collapse of Borders Books

Borders Books Co was established by two bright young men in 1970s; but, in 2012, it unfortunately closed. What has happened with this business? Why did Borders failed while other bookstores such as Barnes & Noble survived? I outline several reasons for this below.

Forty years ago, Borders opened its first store in Ann Arbor, Michigan. The book industry was a different place from our age. People were still reading paper books except e-books. It was not an age of electronic industry in the book world. There was not any kind of outstanding book industry. But there is only Barnes & Noble which was blooming and prospering in the book world. Therefore, couple of young men have established a book store in the name of Borders. However, according to Josh Sanborn, "Borders has been on the verge of insolvency throughout the recession. It briefly flirted with a bid to buy Barnes & Noble (a move most analysts saw as desperate, wrong-headed and financially impossible) and filed to restructure itself under bankruptcy protection laws in February of this same year, when it began closing a third of its then 659 stores."

What was it that forced Borders to write its final chapter? Josh Sanborn[3] describes five reasons as follows:

1. It came too late to the Web. 2. It came too late to e-books. 3. It opened too many stores. 4. It had too much debt. 5. It over-invested in music sales

For years, Borders has opened online book sales to Amazon.com, i.e. visiting borders.com. But it was not a smart management to compete with Barnes & Noble in such a field. And also, Borders didn't foresee the rise of e-books like Amazon and later Barnes & Noble did. It didn't develop its own

e-book customer to compete with the Kindle or the Nook, and Borders only opened an online e-book store one year ago. Opening many stores, Borders began to struggling for how to compete with main line stores and already sinking into water due to over loading in management. For the another reason, Borders has raised $350 million it owed. For two much debt, it could never get out of the hole that it had put itself in by its inefficient business practices.

On the other hand, Borders had heavily invested in music sales in CD sales, iPods, etc. Accordingly, Borders found itself with more expensive retail space than it needed. This put additional pressure on its business model.

What will take Borders place? Although its profits were down late last year, Barnes & Noble remains profitable, there still seems to be a place for traditional bookstores—just of in the size and scope that they were. Last year, the number of independent bookstores in the U.S. actually increased. Increasingly turning to digital books, B&N has avoided that Borders' fate is as the same as tree is falling down due to germ.

There are many important lessons to be learned from the contemporary business world. The company which has a fighting spirit survives in the stormy world, whereas the one does not have strong will power fails in the face of tough competition. The company which has the ability to recognize what is going on in the markets is still standing, but the one which has no awareness of this is forced to close. The one which has appropriate leadership for fighting against waves on the story seas of the commercial world is saved, whereas the one which lacks leadership goes out of business. The company which has a team which can adjust to new challenges keeps its doors open, whereas the one which has no such a leadership vanishes. These are important insights into how to survive in business, and even thrive.

What can leaders of Christian communities learn from this? Where do we stand on Borders or Barnes & Noble? If we are behaving like the former, we will disappear sooner or later. But, with the church, everything is still in place. So, why is it disappearing? What is causing this?

The Bankruptcy of Radio Shack

Founded ninety-four years ago by Theodore and Milton Deutschmann in a storefront in Boston, RadioShack rose to glory with the mass adoption of the radio and the rise of electronics. In 1962, the company was acquired by Tandy Corporation, a New York Stock Exchange-listed, Texas-based leather goods firm that was seeking to diversify; in 2000, the company changed its ticker to RSH.

For ninety-five years, people's lives have been greatly improved by the ready availability of electronics and Radio Shack was at the center of their

mass sales and distribution. Unfortunately, it is announced that it was claiming bankruptcy in February 2015. Many costumers comment as follows.

If RadioShack's demise was inevitable, it was also mourned by the general public. News of the bankruptcy filing prompted an outpouring of memories from one-time Radio Shack customers and tech geeks. Motherboard and the Wall Street Journal were among the outlets for this. They crowd sourced eulogies for the embattled chain: "In the'70s, I saved my allowance and bought a crystal radio set at RadioShack so I could listen to the police calls in San Diego," one reader wrote to the Journal. Another claimed that "RadioShack was the one-stop-shop for everything I needed—PCBs, every type of wire you could imagine, a soldering gun, etc."

In the 1980s, it was still possible to repair consumer electronics is you could obtain the the right parts and had some free time. Today? Good luck. Home-built radios might figure prominently in *All the Light We Cannot See*, but they're far from a typical purchase. More complicated gadgets have also become harder to fidget with. Since 2008, Apple, in particular, has marketed high-end devices that are practically impossible to repair. The last time I bought something at RadioShack was a few years ago—I needed a new battery for my flip phone and couldn't find it on Amazon.

People's fondest memories of RadioShack overwhelmingly involve buying parts to fix and tinker with various electronic devices. This perfectly illustrates why the company has filed for bankruptcy protection. It's going out of business is a sad story. But, what caused it? It helped people to use and enjoy technology, but it seems to have been failed to respond to market conditions and it was not able to adjust to radical changes in technology. Today it has already moved into the field of information technology, but it remains too much of an old-fashioned business and has not been able to catch up new age developments. Finally, 1,700 of its stores will be closed and this means massive job losses.

So, what can we learn from such adverse developments in business? How does this bear on the decline in the church? Unlike business, the church does not have a location problem. But it sometimes does have a problem with lack of leadership and proper management.

The Death of the Green Bay Symphony Orchestra

Symphony is a tremendous musician community which provides a soul bread and harmony to make human spirit move forward. It is true that it has a power to make people rise up from the death again. Green Bay Symphony is one of the mainline music community. However, it was a sad news that the orchestra was filing for bankruptcy. Jesse Rosen, president and CEO of the League of American Orchestras, also believes in the future of American orchestras: "We are experiencing a confluence of changes in cultural and civic priorities, philanthropy, audience preferences and technology," he says. "The combination of all of these factors poses challenges for orchestras, but also opportunities. Many orchestras today are adapting by...experimenting in pricing, concert formats, audience retention strategies, and in artistic and creative innovation."

There are two major symphonies, Milwaukee and Madison. The Madison Symphony Orchestra performs eight programs per season in Overture Hall, and it is managed by veterans of the music scene. Rick Mackie just entered his sixteenth year as executive director, and John DeMain has served as music director for 21 years. Mackie says his time at the MSO has been wonderful due to conductor leadership. Keeping the orchestra healthy in leadership is crucial. DeMain's name recognition is a huge asset for the group, but his leadership skills are valuable as well. As Mackie says. "Be-

Green Bay Symphony's closing is a wake-up call for groups in Madison and beyond

cause John [DeMain] is a conductor who behaves appropriately and professionally with the musicians, the relationship is warm and respectful. We all get along."

"We're a model orchestra," DeMain says. "Other orchestras should study us." As for breaking down barriers, Mackie says "The main reason for any orchestra to exist is to build a better community," says Mark Cantrell, the WCO's executive director. "If the organization truly understands why it exists and [knows] its values, it gives a strong, enduring foundation to build upon."

What can we, as a church community, learn from the collapse of Green Bay Symphony? The lack of leadership and management contributed to this disaster. There were problems with insufficient financing, an aging audience, lack of performers, etc. The leaders all failed to manage the organization in keeping with the radical changes that are going on in society. The leaders followed the status quo and clung to routine ways for bringing in funds when the really needed to work on doing a full court press, as we say in basketball. They really did not foresee the adverse developments that eventually occurred. If today's church operates like the Green Bay Symphony did, it, too, will soon be facing bankruptcy.

Jesus in Starbucks

It is amazing! I see Jesus in Starbucks Coffee Shop in New York and other places as well. He is leading forum with people. What is that?

In "Transforming His Company"⁴ Starbucks CEO Howard Schultz stated that the company's coffee is now well known as one of the best and priciest coffee shops in the world. Since it started in Seattle in 1971, it has grown tremendously and now has nearly 12,000 stores nationwide. The Schultz Family Foundation has trained nearly 700 disadvantaged workers for jobs in retail and customer service. And, Time states, "Howard Schultz isn't afraid of his feelings. Or anybody else's, for that matter" in tenuous conditions. For example, he has pledged to hire 10,000 military veterans by the end of 2018. Schultz has promised to offer tuition for full and part-time Starbucks employees who are working toward a bachelor's degree. And, he takes a creative approach to management. He has created a set of premium stores and has also increased the number of faster, on-the-go locations. Certain reserve locations will serve the company's top-of-the-line roast. As Rana Foroohar notes, Starbucks is also planning to expand its quick-turnaround business in locations like coffee trucks and stores built out of shipping containers.

Thus, the company is truly on the way to transforming of itself, toward becoming a community store, a sort of *Gemeinschaft* rather than a *Gesellschaft*. Furthermore, Starbucks is on solid ground with Schultz's social and political commitments: "Shocked by recent police shootings and unrest in Ferguson, MO...he decided to hold open meetings in five cities where Starbucks employees from top managers to entry-level baristas could speak frankly about their experiences with racism. On an icy January afternoon in New York 2015, Schultz was leading a forum on race." At the forum, the people agreed that "We are at a tipping point" in America. Schultz's social concern is most noticeably where the problems of student debt, health care, veterans' rights, youth unemployment and gun violence are concerned. As Ms. Foroohar observed, he told *Time* that this could change your local Starbucks as you know it. These changes also reflect the challenges facing the country as a whole. "Whether you're a Republican or a Democrat," he recently said, "we can all know and recognize one thing: the country is not going in the right direction."⁵ Ms. Foroohar also states that, "Schultz has worried about the effects of partisan politics on the economy. He is deeply invested in these ideas not only because making the company a preferred employer helps keep turnover costs lower and service quality higher than the industry average, but also because he believes corporations have a duty to help people realize the American Dream."⁶

Schultz's forum is actually amazing in so far as it brought up so many important ideas for transforming America through his employees and the company's customers. Normally, business is a place for develop economically, and this development is usually taken to be based on capital alone. But Schultz, he who is a business man, has managed this forum on socio-political issues very skillfully and in such a ways that it can indeed contribute to moving America in the right direction. Schultz has had a great impact to the current society, and under tenuous conditions. I think that Starbucks will never die because its leader is focused on taking care of human beings. That is, I see Jesus at the Starbucks.

I would pose a serious question to Christian leaders: Do you not thing that Starbucks is taking on role normally played by the church? Is the church moving into the Starbucks? Is it over there, namely at Starbucks? Who moved Jesus into the Starbucks? Is your church still in its usual location? Do you see Jesus in it? If you do, then your church will not face decline.

In relation to this story about Starbucks, Thom & Joani Schultz, author of *Why Nobody Wants to Go to Church Anymore,* suggest a sort of *café ministry* in a new mode of faith expression and a different way of doing church. As they note, "75% say they sense that God is motivating people to say stay connected with Him, but in different ways and through different types of experiences than in the past."[7] The authors try to identify the church with Starbucks in so far as people are perfectly comfortable inviting friends there for coffee and conversation.

In conclusion, most of the opinions concerning today's church and its efficacy in the community seem to be moving in a direction that is directly opposed to church policy They say that the leadership of the church is unqualified and that they have separated themselves from the church's real needs. They don't seem to have a sense of co-operation. The pastor and the lay people are going in opposite directions, sometimes working directly against each other. There is a lack of willingness on the part of the leadership to address what is going on in the world. Every day is changing into a political and economic tempest. A crisis is brewing in and around the church, but its leaders are desensitized to it and lacking in any true crisis consciousness. Therefore, they don't know what to do and or what they have to do. And, this is the cause of the decline. So, will the church finally be able to listen to the thinking outlined here and correct its course?

NOTES

1. Alvin Toffler, *The Third Wave*, William Morrow and Co. NY, NY, 1980. p. XX
2. Young J. Choe, *Authentic Pastor, Authentic Leadership.* Lanham, MD. Hamilton Books, 2012. p. 8.
3. I described the death of Borders based on a comment of Josh Sanborn who is a business commentator for *Time* Magazine, http://business.time.com/2011/07/19/5-reasons-borders-went-out-of-business-and-what-will-take-its-place/
4. *Time* Magazine, Feb 16, 2015, by Rana Foroohar.
5. Ibid, p. 20.
6. Ibid, p. 21.
7. Thom & Joani Schultz, *Why Doesn't Anybody Want to go to Church Anymore?* pp. 59-60. For further details, see *Cafe Ministry.* pp. 57-61.

Chapter Five

The Sunday Pastor and the Everyday Pastor

In its early chapters, this book has focused on the cause of decline in the church. It identified the Sunday pastor as one of these causes. What is it about his or her leadership that is causing this? This chapter focuses on

today's image of a pastor in the midst of the declining church. It explores two types, namely the *Sunday Pastor* and *Everyday Pastor*.

WHO IS THE SUNDAY PASTOR?

Who is the Sunday pastor? He is invisible and paralyzed. He is appointed to the local church by the bishop. However, the congregations don't seem to see him as their pastor in the everyday ministry. The pastor does not show up and perform the tasks of the ministry. He is almost a stranger to the congregation because of the separation that exists between him and others in the community. He is not a member of the community family, but seems like a guest or visitor because he does not even know where the people live or who they are. Sometimes people stand together, but they are like oil and water—they don't mix. Again, such a pastor remains completely segregated from the community and so basically off track where responsibilities are concerned. He may show up only at the Sunday service, preach only with his or her lips and then collect a salary. This is called being a Sunday pastor. If the Sunday pastor does not come to the church on weekdays, where is he? What is he doing? Sleeping? Sick? Babysitting? Going golfing or fishing? Or debauching himself?

In another way, he or she seems like a "poli-pastor" (political pastor) who is wandering around the meetings looking for a higher position and promotion toward bishop and district superintendent. For the poli-pastor, political gain is a priority rather than taking care of the local church. Therefore, their daily schedules are full of more outside meetings rather than the church ministry. For this reason, today's church is falling into decline.

The Sunday pastor is also described in John 10: 11-14. According to Jesus, there are two types of shepherds. The Sunday pastor is a hired hand. Jesus preaches to him or her as follows.

> I am the good shepherd. The good shepherd lays down his life for the sheep. The hired hand is not the shepherd who owns the sheep. So when he sees the wolf coming, he abandons the sheep and runs away. Then the wolf attacks the flock and scatters it. The man runs away because he is a hired hand and cares nothing for the sheep.

This message was aimed at the Jewish religious leaders who were working around the Temple. They had exploited the people who came to worship. They craftily oppressed them by producing six hundred twenty Old Testament laws. The people were forced by the corrupt desires of their leader to live in keeping with these laws. When the worshippers brought their offerings to the altar and these offerings were disqualified so that the Temple leaders could co-opt them and make use of them themselves. But, the people had brought their valuable offerings to God, not to the clergy. This kind of the immoral behavior was going on even in the time of Jesus. Such a clever leader is, however, only a hired hand. This is why Jesus said, "You are making a den of thieves of the house of God."(Mk. 11: 11-14). Such blasphemy is perhaps explainable historically, but it is still morally problematic. So, the Jewish religious communities also had the equivalent of Sunday pastors.

Today the Sunday pastor comes to the church as God's servant. But he does not fit the image of a legitimate servant of God. Instead, he is more like a job seeker, someone who is only looking to collect a salary from the church and to avoid communal obligations. The congregation is likely working hard at supporting every aspect of the ministry, but the Sunday pastor is looking for looks a salary and a pension. Therefore, he does not demonstrate a sense of calling from God. This is why some congregations call the Sunday pastor a hired man, not an appointed one.

I have known Dong-Soo Lee, a pastoral friend who is always available to talk. We have talked about the calling to serve God and we agree that, when Korea was under Japanese colonial domination, it was possible to find people there who had a clear calling to God or the nation, a commitment to a religious and national liberation movement. But it is hard to find anything like such a calling in today's church because today's pastor is merely an office holder and a professional job seeker. Theological knowledge is only requirement for getting into the church. The fact that one has a call to serve God does not really matter. It is thus that the spiritual power of the church is being sapped.

Today's congregations have a question to answer. Why do we have to feed and care for the Sunday pastor? Would the church not perhaps be better off without him? The latest trend is for the church to support itself by relying on a lay speaker only. The age of the Sunday pastor must be end and a new age of truly engaged Christian leadership must begin. We need to practice a priesthood of the whole person, instead of that of the Sunday pastor.

If the Sunday pastor continues to behave as he does in the community, it will become apparent that he is a fraud and a thief. Such pastors do not have an honest relation to God. They have a minimal commitment to the work of the ministry and are like the hired hand who "...is not the shepherd who owns the sheep. So when he sees the wolf coming, he abandons the sheep and runs away . . . ". Accordingly, the judgment of God is at hand. His rage is waiting for them. They are only attending upon their own destruction and even devastation. The church is being killed by their cheating and self-centeredness.

If the Sunday pastor is a sluggard and a thief, then how can we drive him out of the community? I call upon the Conference leadership to supervise and correct this problem with a vehemence and a marked change in policy. First, the congregations need to report such problems to the Bishop and Superintendents. The Conference should make them stop to practicing the ministry. And then, the offending pastors must attend a class aimed at correcting these problems —until they undergo a personal transformation. And, they should not be given a new appointment until their problematic behavior has totally changed. They don't deserve to continue to benefit in any way from the church.

THE EVERYDAY PASTOR SAVES THE CHURCH

Who is the Everyday Pastor? As Jesus said, "I lay down my life for the sheep. I have other sheep that are not of this sheep pen. I must bring them also, they too will listen to my voice, and there shall be one flock and one shepherd." (John 10: 15-16).

We recognize that Jesus' audience was the Jewish religious society. The hired hand runs away from crises crisis, i.e., the wolf comes and threatens the sheep and he disappears. However, the good shepherd lays down his life for the people. This message unfortunately reflects the troubled nature of Jewish religious community life in the time of Jesus. For the good shepherd, the church is not a steppingstone or bridge to a better position. "Lay down my life for the sheep" means total commitment to God's Will rather than my own. It shows a sense of responsibility and a caring spirit, a will to protect the community against evil. It is the essence of surrender to God with mind and spirit.

Hence the true nature of the Everyday pastor evidences itself in his ministry. He or she does represent the true image of Jesus. The Everyday pastor is never aloof or segregated from the community, because he is willing to engage every aspect of the ministry. He is hard working day and night beyond his required hours and salary, because he is not an employee who works for time and money. He is a farmer in the garden of the Kingdom and works for the glory of God. Even though he is hard working, his shoulders are light with joy and happiness. The pastor and congregations share a togetherness as a family members, both sufferings and joys, struggles and rewards. This builds and deepens the bond of trust between them.

Furthermore, the Everyday pastor takes care of the other sheep. He tends to everyone who is struggling in this troubled world and is therefore social and ethically responsible. Isaiah 62: 1 is his watchword: "For Zion's sake I will not keep silent, for Jerusalem's sake I will not remain quiet, till her righteousness shines out like the dawn her salvation like a blazing torch."

In the Gospel of John, Jesus was filled with concern for the other sheep pen. As John Wesley said, "The world is my parish." These are the ideals of a good shepherd. The Everyday pastor sets such standards for himself. He looks beyond the confines of the church and casts his eyes outward to the troubled world. As the Bible is concerned about the world, so he, too, is no stranger to human misery and speaks and works for love and justice. He never allows evil to gain a foothold in his community—or anywhere he goes. He never keeps silent in the face of injustice and suffering. He cries out for the righteousness of the Kingdom of God on earth and clearly has a goal to achieve. He is indeed a visionary, someone who is hopeful and envisions a humane future for mankind.

The everyday pastor is welcomed by the congregation. Let me introduce an example of a pastor who was in charge of a three point church in Wisconsin. The pastor spent equal time at each church during the week. Stopping at each one was an opportunity for the parishioners to meet with him. The everyday pastor liked to set up a New Year's breakfast for the council members at a restaurant in order to offer New Year's greetings and blessings. And, he and his wife regularly invited the entire congregations to the annual meal table at the church. This included some of the town people who were now on friendly terms. And, this is the same practice as Jesus set up—breaking bread together. His banquets were, however, at the table of the Kingdom of God. Whenever the pastor had an opportunity to eat together with parishioners, he would pay the bills ahead of time at the restaurant. He liked to treat people. This made their relationship stable and strong and the result was a friendship of trust.

One night, something great happened at the parsonage. After dinner, almost the entire congregation came unannounced to visit the pastor, because it was his birthday. They tried to create a surprise party and brought him many gifts. How wonderfully they loved each other! It was a fantastic event for all of them. It proved that he was the Everyday pastor and that he had a genuine calling from God. He was the man who had surrendered to God. Under such leadership, there is no reason for the church to decline. Wherever he goes, the Everyday pastor saves the church.

In conclusion, the Sunday pastor disqualifies himself from service to the church even though he was appointed to a community by a bishop. He has no a right to expect a monthly salary from the church. But, the Sunday pastor also has to be mindful of the following:

"Not everyone who says to me, Lord, Lord will enter the kingdom of heaven, but only he who does the will of my Father who is in heaven . . . Then I will tell them plainly, 'I never knew you away from me, you evildoers!'" (Matt. 7: 21-23).

In the Parable of the sons (Matt. 21: 28-32), the second son answered 'I will, sir,' but he did not go. "Which of the two did what his father wanted?" The second failed to go to the vineyard. For the second son, Jesus says that "the tax collectors and prostitutes are entering eh kingdom of God ahead of you." (31vs). In the Parable of the Talents, Jesus gave a severe word to the one talent, "And throw that worthless servant outside, into the darkness, where there will be weeping and gnashing of teeth. (Matt. 25: 30). Thus, the Sunday pastor is a target of blame according to Jesus. He or she receives nothing but judgment.

However, to the Everyday pastor, Jesus says *"Well done, good and faithful servant! You have been faithful with a few things; I will put you in charge of many things. Come and share your master's happiness!" (Matt. 25: 21).* Therefore, he or she is a true shepherd rather than a pastor and a disciple of Jesus as a company for the Kingdom journey together.

This chapter is seriously concerned with a difference between a biblical shepherd and an institutional pastor. The shepherd stands for the lambs unconditionally beyond a base of job. But the pastor accounts his own benefit more than the lambs. For this reason, the shepherd saves the church, but the pastor may destroy the church. Who is a shepherd today? It is hard to see a true shepherd rather than a pastor. Pastor looks for a career and benefit chance. But shepherd lay down his life to the lambs and to solve the world issues. In the beginning, Jesus wanted a shepherd, not a pastor.

Chapter Six

The Healthy Lay and Church Disruptor

The time of Jesus was troubled and marked by socio-political and religious fragmentation. People were dehumanized, turned against love, justice, and human rights. So the Bible says that it was a dark age. People were oppressed

and exploited by political and religious forces greater than themselves. It is for this reason that Jesus said in the Gospel of Matthew (Matt. 7: 15-20),

> Watch out for false prophets. They come to you in sheep's clothing, but inwardly they are ferocious wolves. By their fruit you will recognize them do people pick grapes from thorn bushes, or figs from thistles? Likewise every good tree bears good fruit, but a bad tree bears bad fruit. A good tree cannot bear bad fruit, and a bad tree cannot bear good fruit. Every tree that does not bear good fruit is cut down and thrown into the fire. Thus, by their fruit you will recognize them.

Thus, sometimes, the church is a place of wolves. They are hidden behind the curtains. There may be ferocious wolves who look for opportunity to attack the pastor and the people. And, a bad tree bears bad fruit. These people are involved with plots to undermine the church and set fire to it. But, sometimes even such people are baptized; they can even be elected members of the church council. But they are not working for the church. Their only goal is satisfaction of their egotistical and selfish needs. They seek to use human desire to destroy the church—power games and group dynamics which place control in their hands. And, often there are a number of bad trees and fruits in the community. This makes it hard to claim that the church is angelic or divine community.

CONFLICTS INTERNAL TO THE CHURCH

Is the church a place of angels? Is it the place of love and righteousness that Jesus sought to establish? Many churches try to achieve this. Biblically and theologically, the divine mandate is to bring about the Kingdom of God. The substance of the message might be correct, but the reality on the ground is often quite different. It is for this reason that I wrote the following:

> The church is not only a peace center but also a conflict center. There are many negatives that can possibly turn into trouble under a pastor's leadership. And, church communities contain different types of people who understand each other differently in terms of family background, education, social status, health condition, relationship, and person. Some of them also looked at things from a different angle biblically and theologically. Such a human tendencies make each crisis both frightening and potentially destructive.

The conflicts in the church amount to a dangerous disease that undermines the community, like a cancer, a chronic malady.

GROUP GAMES AND POWER GAMES

There was a church in mid-Wisconsin which had been struggling for a long time. It closed due to internal conflicts. There were two groups in the church fighting for their own egotistical interests. They were struggling with the issue of place was where to set up the church and national flags. One group wanted to set up the church flag on the right side of the altar, and the other wanted it on the left. The location of these flags was important for each group and this devolved into a power game within the church. But Biblically and theologically we cannot find any rule which states where the flags should be placed. Pure selfishness was what was was motivating both groups. And, they never overcame the gulf of this conflict. Finally, and tragically, the church split into two parts. It was effectively destroyed due to human arrogance and belligerence.

CONTROLLING BEHAVIORS

Controlling behavior is a dangerous and can bring about the destruction of the church, wherever it is subject to internal stresses. Usually one or two families try to control the community by their money, social background, number, etc. They are the mainstream of the church and control the Pastor Parish Relationship Committee, Nomination Committee, Finance Committee, etc. For this reason, the church cannot be run democratically or on the basis of equality and generosity. Some people seem to become slaves to the church leadership. But this does not make for a healthy church community. Instead, it works against growth and then finally the church vanishes. In many towns, small churches are often riddled with such controlling behaviors. The church community is too small to keep the healthy members from being defeated by such controlling behavior. Like the human body, the church needs a healthy cells to create muscles and boost its strength.

UNHEALTHY PEOPLE AS ROTTEN APPLES

When I was appointed to a Caucasian church in Wisconsin I unfortunately had a very difficult experience. As a new pastor, I was coming to a parish which was completely unknown to me and in a remote area. One of the church members said that the new pastor who is coming was his enemy. This was shocking and gave me a deep sense of disappointment. The reason was supposedly that he had once gone to an Asians country for military service. He had had a bad experience with Asian people when he had served there. He was blamed and suffered as a result of their behaviors. So he was looking for revenge. Finally, my appointment to the church was a great chance for him to

get his revenge on me. That's why he said that his enemy was coming to my church.

My ministry there began with a stranger who was waiting for me, anticipating that I was his enemy. He always complained about my leadership and moved the community to sedition. He was a member of the church council, but he never attended worship service until I left the church. By contrast to this, I had never missed a Council meeting, even though I had to listen to his complaints.

One day I was threatened by his brutal blasphemy. I made the mistake of mispronouncing his name. His first name was "Jon." He said "Jahn," but I said "Jon." He got angry and said "Get out of here!" Needless to say, this created a major headache for me and made me miserable during the time period of my ministry.

However, one of the faithful members approached me with a word: "He is a rotten apple. Don't pay attention to him!" When I left the church, he had passed away. How can we help such people?

My suggestion is to discuss such matters with the Superintendent. He should call the man and guide him in grace and peace psychologically and biblically. The Superintendent (or Circuit meeting) also needs to support the pastor, they need to watch and listen to the voice of struggle from him. Who is undermining the church? If individuals do something bad, bishop and superintendent need to guide them to be transformed in a gracious way.

SOME CHURCHES IN HUMAN HANDS

It is seriously dangerous when the church is in the hands of individuals who become involved in plots and intrigue. If such things are left unchecked, the church will quickly careen toward its own destruction. And, sometimes, things do not go well for a church if it is administered by committees. Some of them exceed their boundaries and violate social rules. Consider the case of a superintendent who has tried to manage the church on the basis of 'intelligence' that a church insider has provided. If the Superintendent needs to know what is going on in the church, he calls upon such a man. Thus he has trusted him in preference to the pastor. He was empowered and treated as a special person by the superintendent. So he was prideful. He has tried to control the pastor. He has acted out his own urge to power. So the church will actually be controlled by the interactions of these two individuals, and not by the church council. Needless to say, none of the superintendents needs a spy.

When a church has been subject to such human plots and intrigues, it inevitably grows weaker and weaker. Some of the members leave because of the lack of authentic leadership. And, some Superintendents unconditionally stand by lay people whenever conflicts happen. In troubled times, a Superintendent may even send the pastor to a counselor or seminary class. This is hardly a right decision since it does not promote a win-win situation. Superintendent needs to deal with them equally. They need a gracious teaching and guidance rather than punishment. The superintendent needs labor to serve grace rather than do a paper work for assigning punishment.

Such a proud man tried to take control in my church community. He wanted to be a representative of the church. For this reason, he tried to manage the pastor's office. That's why he has suggested the pastor his office to that in the parsonage. Some of pastors do set up their offices there, but this is actually not proper. The parsonage is a private location, it serves for the activities of daily life. By contrast, the church office is a public place. It is from there that one can most effectively represent the church. The pastor needs to keep his dignity and he can best do this by working from the public office. If lay people need an office, they can to set up one at another location in the church. Everybody needs to acknowledge boundaries.

In the resolution of church conflicts, the superintendent needs a pastoral handbook in order to transform and guide the church toward grace and peace. The superintendent does not need to have a game going on on the side, nor does he need to choose between the pastor and the lay person(s). What is necessary is equal treatment of both parties rather than punishment of either.

And, lastly, to acquire skills in conflict resolution, people need to attend a special workshop with the superintendent.

A HOMOGENEOUS CHURCH

Some churches belong to a type of homogeneous community where race, tradition, clan, social relationships, etc. are concerned. Some are dominated by family lines. Some are collecting places for close friends, school mates, and hometown mates. Some churches find that racial conflicts develop due to concentrations of one or another group. The homogeneous church is not healthy, however, because it is not open. This is one of the causes of decline in the church.

Chapter Seven

Twenty Four Ideas for Restoring the Church

MISSION STATEMENT

We aim to restore the church and society through transformation leadership and to support local and global communities in this.

The purpose of this book is to focus on the serious decline in the church and to offer at least some ideas as to how to restore it. These ideas have been put into practice and explored through ministry with pastoral colleagues and congregations for a long time. Every situation of ministry is different, but it

is my hope that these ideas can be made to apply in any church where there is enthusiasm and decisiveness. If we say things are "impossible," then surely nothing will happen. But if we say they are "possible", then at least something will happen. We are reminded of the Jesus' words:

> Everything is possible for him who believes. (Mark 9: 23)
> And:
> If anyone says to this mountain 'Go throw yourself into the sea, and does not doubt in his heart but believes that what he says will happen, it will be done for him. (Mark 11: 23).

Thus, believing makes things happen. And, great things will happen if we try. Effort is key. If we don't try, nothing will happen. The following ideas are intended to help leaders who are struggling with decline in their churches and working toward restoration. The programs can be carried out in any church community where people come together.

SOME PROGRAMS THAT CAN AFFECT A TURNAROUND IN THE CHURCH

Church Transformation Workshop

This workshop deals with "Making disciples for Jesus and the transformation of the world." It is intended to help the church make a turnaround and move toward revitalization in the midst of decline. The workshop offers the chance for people to express their dreams and visions, identify the contradictions that underlie their thinking, draft proposals, workout strategies and tactics, and develop timelines. It requires 4 to 5 hours on a weekday or Sunday and takes place at the church with congregation, pastors, staff, and representatives of the Transformation Leadership School (TLS)

Transformation Leadership Seminar

This helps pastors, teachers, managers, CEOs, and employees who need a transformative community in order to have a meaningful life and maximize their talents and potential in the work place. It aims to teach transformation leadership by drawing on the liberal arts and to thereby enhance people's cultural life. In the process, vertical leadership becomes horizontal leadership. This seminar centers on a community of togetherness, not a solo leadership. It takes about 5-6 hours on a weekday or a weekend and at a chosen place.

Four Steps to Transformation: Realizing the Kingdom of God

The Bible is a book of transformation. This is its key subject—the Kingdom of God as introduced by Jesus. But the historical church has distorted the authentic message of Jesus and has come to be centered on ritual worship instead. This program focuses on how a person can be transformed. It identifies four steps: Spiritual Transformation, Personal Transformation, Transformation of Disciples, and Social Transformation. This gets at the substance of Jesus' message and it is opposed to its institutionalization. The seminar takes about two hours, though the time can be extended.

Transformation Retreat for Congregations and Employees

This retreat helps congregations and employees who want to enhance their lives and be transformed by Jesus' key message of the Kingdom of God. One can expect to experience a renewal of one's life, a shift from the old into the new, at this Christ-centered retreat. It includes lectures, discussion, and group workshops which introduce and promote this transformation. The time allotted for this event is one day or two days including an overnight.

Back to America Movement, USA

In this global age, America seems to have lost the image of a model country. This seminar aims to help American people restore their authentic sense of value, spirit, and morality. Church and community will need to set up a small group to launch the movement in conjunction with TLS leaders. The following are the necessary steps for this:

- Love your Country: America has been the world ideal and a dream destination for over a century.
- Understand the origins of democracy.
- Keep your American values, spirit, and identity.
- Don't depend on the government unnecessarily.
- Keep the public environment clean.
- Keep your behavior good in public and under all conditions.
- Be honest: Keep your moral standards high.
- Present a good appearance. Americans should set the example for others.
- Bring back "Made in America."
- Get back to church as it is a center of spiritual growth.

The Five "Less" Movements

Many contemporary people are promoting invaluable lifestyle changes with their concerns about global warming, health, environment, and global security. This seminar centers on human and global health and well being as the principle and basis of order in God's creation. It will be developed through small group activity, and will include a campaign and rally in the community. The following are ways of doing "less" of certain things. They conduce to better overall health of both individuals and community, are so are recommended for seminar participants:

- Eat less Salt
- Eat less Sugar
- Do not speed when driving
- Generate less waste and recycle wherever possible
- Stop smoking

The Twelve-Step Pre-Marital Class

This seminar is intended to assist pre-marital singles and couples who have previously sought only guidelines on preparation for marriage that focus on its material aspects. Participants will learn about the importance of personal transformation before they enter into marriage. Preparing for marriage by focusing only on the material aspects of a couple's future life amounts to building on sand. Instead, they need to make it a priority to know who they are as individuals, where they come from spiritually and culturally, and whether they are compatible with each other.

Transformation Couple Enrichment Programs

Transformation Couple Enrichment is a positive experience for married couples who are seeking to deepen and enhance their relationships with each other and with God. This is a wonderful weekend for them and an opportunity to get away from jobs, family, chores, phones and email and to focus only on each other. If you would like greater depth, growth and enrichment in your relationship, this marriage enrichment seminar can make a difference for you.

Principles and Practice of Transformation Preaching

For the preacher, the ultimate destination is to know God's will by turning away from my own. This requires that one take responsibility for discerning and deliver the substantial message of transformation through belief in, and commitment to, the Kingdom of God to the people. This seminar takes three hours per day and runs for eight weeks.

Projecting a Fantastic Image: Image Design and Consultation

The twenty-first century is the time for imaging. A quality image gives us competitive power in navigating relationships at work and in public. Human beauty comes from bodily health, beauty of mind, an inspiring spirit, and a clean soul. This seminar teaches participants how to develop a better image for a more successful life, one lived in joy and happiness. Participants are recommended to take the full course, which lasts 5-6 hours.

Cultural-Educational Lectures

This is an opportunity for people to improve their knowledge and understanding of local and global issues in a variety of ways. It is also helpful for people who wish to enrich their lives, spirits, and sense of values. These sessions will involve well-known speakers on diverse subjects.

Forum for Church and Society in a Global Context

People need to know what is going on and what to do in our radically and rapidly changing world. This is an open lecture with a seminar and also includes debate for those concerned with local and global issues. It provides an opportunity for people to talk and exchange ideas so as to make better moral and ethical decisions. It teaches people to stand, and speak, for love and justice in a troubled world and takes place in a small group setting.

Youth and Children Crystal Bell Choir

- *Purpose:* To bring the young and their parents and others to the church through the Youth Choir and Children activity.
- *Reward*: Conference and churches should provide scholarships for young people who take part in the Music Ministry.
- *How to organize?:* Conference and Circuit should encourage local churches to organize teams for developing Youth Choir as well as Children's Choir.

How can we fill the empty church? Youth and Children's choirs are one of the best programs for restoring the declining church. Youth and children definitely bring their parents and neighbors when they perform the music at the church. Parents like to recognize their kids' activities. They never make excuses when it comes to going to church when music programs are running.

In particular, the Children's Crystal Bell Choir is a fantastic addition to the worship service and makes a noticeable impact on the congregation. The cost for any instrument is about $300.00. For the Crystal Bell Choir, the church needs to recruit children from the community through advertising.

This will have a great effect on the community and will serve as its best outreach program.

Let me share a story about what happened at Lowell United Methodist Church with the Children's Crystal Bell Choir. I encouraged the Sunday School to launch it. The two teachers decided to purchase a basic set of Crystal Bells for $ 300.00 using the Sunday School budget. They organized two children and four adults for the beginning performance. The four adults were called upon because there were not enough children in the church. The first performance was successful and a fantastic addition to the worship service. The sound of the music brought feelings of joy and happiness to the listeners. The Crystal Choir has continued to perform on Sundays and other occasions.

A similarly wonderful thing happened at the Christmas Eve Service. Now the Children's Crystal Bell Choir consists of six children and no adults. They have brought parents, grandparents, friends and neighbors to the Christmas Eve worship service. The performance of Crystal Bell Choir was amazing and .attendance averaged 25 adults and children on Sunday. But the evening worship service was full. The church is located in a small town with a population of only 430 people. However, I see great hope that the church can make a turn around.

Reinventing Vacation Bible School

Traditionally Vacation Bible School has been one of the representative Christian educational programs in the community. In previous decades, it was a fantastic vacation program aimed at helping children who need a faith experience combined with fun at the church. But many of the churches can no longer run VBS due to lack of leadership, money, and human resources. Where this is the case, a church may need to make requests to a bigger church for assistance with the operation of such a school.

Today many children are abandoned on the streets. And also, many seem to be obsessed with electronic technology. This means exposure to social hazards as well as social alienation. Children need spiritual nourishment in the midst of tribulations of this world. While VBS is running, the church can call parents to a meeting so that they can also participate in such a ministry.

Vacation Bible School is one of the best programs the children's ministry. But, as noted, many churches are not able to open such programs due to financial limitations and lack of available leadership in the summer. To solve these problems, a small sized church needs to submit a proposal for assistance from a neighboring, larger church. They have budgets for outreach ministry.

When I was at one of the three point churches, I requested help from The Korean United Methodist Church in Minnesota in opening a VBS. At the time, they were planning to send resources to a Mexican ministry. But they changed their plan and came to our church. They prepared everything they needed by way of leadership, materials, resources, food, and money. The VBS team consisted of thirteen young teachers and three adult teachers. They served very well, working for three years day and night and sleeping in the church basement. When they had finished the class work in the morning, in the afternoon they went out preaching and witnessing on the streets and knocking on the doors.

So, if, when performing the ministry, we say something is impossible, it won't happen. But if we say things are possible, everything can happen. My wife Prisca has directed me to change the word *impossible* into *I am possible*. Consider the words of Confucius: *Everything is possible. But it is has not happened, because we do not think it so.*

Anybody for Music?

Music touches the soul. Human beings are actually enormously conflicted and complicated because they are different ideologically, socio-culturally, and mentally. It is difficult to unify them, to find common ground. However, music makes them come together, in spite of different languages and customs. For this reason, it is a good idea for the church to set up seasonal concerts for the community. They will serve as a bridge to the world.

Open House for the Community

What does this consist of?

- Eating together, e.g. potluck suppers
- Fellowship—a chance to get to know people in the community
- Praying together about concerns of the church and community.
- Learning together from medical doctors, nurses, school principals and teachers, police officers, mayors, EMT staff, fireman, businessmen, etc.
- Musical performances

When does this take place? Every Wednesday at 6:00 P.M.
   Where does it meet? All of the churches.

Learning from a Model Church

If we are truly eager to restore and revitalize the church, we ought to learn about a model church which is growing in a healthy way, and then ask\ how this is happening. What is the reason? Is the leadership different from that of others? What programs make the church grow? We need to identify and study such churches throughout the world. We need to visit with their pastors, staff, and congregations and then set up a meeting for evaluation and organize a taskforce to direct it. For a model church, there are some elements of greatness is in spirit and organization and these cause growth.

Fusion Ministry: A Multi-Racial Approach

Today we are entering upon a new global age that is vastly different from the previous one in many ways, one of them being the increasingly multi-racial nature of communities. America is already becoming a collecting place for hundreds of different races. Homogenous culture and community no longer exist in this land. The new wave of heterogeneous people is having a continual and marked effect on the nation's demographic. According to current data, white people will no longer be in the majority in American society after 2020 of 2030. Latinos and African-Americans will predominate. Therefore, a monochromatic ministry is no longer fitting, nor can it contribute to the growth of the church. The church needs to pay attention to other races in addition to continuing to work on its existing ministry. This new development might be called a Fusion Ministry, a bit like a business which sells books and coffee together.

The Talk-Talk Meeting

The term Talk-Talk Meeting refers to a gathering of people who are concerned about personal issues questions of faith, church, the well being of society and the world. These are opportunities for leaders who want to express and discuss their opinions in public. Still, it is hard to find lay people who have a desire to express such life concerns and talk about such issues. So, there is need for a regular meetings. Coffee and food at the church are also a good idea in conjunction with these meetings. In some cases, participants may discuss and forward their agendas and suggestions to local governments.

The Open-Window Church

What I am here terming an open-window church attempts to combine parts of traditional worship with the forum on world issues. According to Karl Barth, church leaders need to take the Bible in one hand and the newspaper in the other. This makes for dialogue and communal connection. An open-window church continues to engage in prayer, sing hymns, listen to preaching, and make offerings. But it may also participate in forums on racism, gun violence, healthcare, immigration, terrorism, government, international affairs, etc. As for these forums, this worship style invites professional leaders from the community to speak on various subjects. An open-window church declares that the church is tasked with taking care of the community. It makes the church a player in the progress of history. Jesus came to fix our broken world. The Bible talks about this, but today's church does not deal with the broken world. More often, it ignores it. But an open-window church is a two-sided coin: It is committed to both worship and addressing social issues.

Outreach Ministry

Who is the ideal leader, the individual who can be productive for a growing church? Is he merely an office holder? A Sunday pastor? Honestly, such people are one of the causes of decline in the church. I would like to share Jesus' words at this point. Recall his statement, "Go to the fence and bring the people right away. Fill my house." (Luke 11). The death or growth of the church derives from its pastoral leadership. A fisherman goes to a lake if he wants fish; a farmer goes to a farm if he wants grow crops; an employee goes to a company if he wants money and food. So, the pastor needs to go into the streets. This is where the people are waiting to hear the message, where the lost sheep are wandering around. To sustain the church, go door to door and knock.

When I was serving at a small church in northern Wisconsin, one family had been broken up due to divorce. The wife and children had left the husband alone at their former home. He was a farmer who never came to church. His house was located on the hillside near a local highway. I drove there on a weekly basis. One day he was working in his field and I called to him, "Hi, Jim! Come to the church!" He came on next the Sunday and is still serving faithfully in an administrative position.

The second story happened at the church parsonage in where I am now living. One day, a family moved into the village near my home. I decided to visit them with flowers. We shared a greeting and welcomed them to the village. I never said "Come and join the church!" I just greeted the family. Later they joined the church. They like to attend the services and Sunday Bible study and bring their grandchildren. The children also play in the Children's Bell Choir on occasion. They are already settled down as steady members in a stable relationship with the church.

A restaurant is one of the best places for reaching out to people. It is a good place to learn who is who. The pastor and church members need to take the opportunity to meet people and engage them at any place and any time. Some people are waiting for a handshake, someone to welcome and to guide them. They need encouragement. Nobody knows who is waiting for our open hands, so we need make the best of every opportunity. Trying makes something happen. An invitation to join in a meal is also good.

Jesus said, "I am your friend." Friendship helps relationships develop properly as it deepens understanding. Many things can contribute to the development of friendships, one of them is enjoying a meal together. Church leaders need to invite people to the parsonage or meet with them at restaurants, or, talk with them on special occasions such as weddings, funerals, etc.

The Story of Spurgeon (1834-1892)[1]

Charles H. Spurgeon developed his ministry into a powerful prayer group. According to one record, two hundred people supported it in prayer every day. John Wesley, founder of Methodism, prayed three times per day. He sought to e strength to It defeat evil. There are of the many same types of leading personalities in other spiritual traditions.

One particularly powerful story from Spurgeon comes to mind immediately. He liked to go to the train station where he would wait for people who needed a ride. If he found someone who did, he was willing to help them get wherever they needed to go. The important thing is that Spurgeon preached during the ride. He led them to return to Jesus Christ.

This may seem like an old fashion story, but he is still an inspiration and a powerful stimulus for outreach. Today we, pastors and people, talk Jesus Christ only in the context of our one-hour worship service, not on the streets and in public. The result is that He becomes the man who is only present inside the church, around the altar.

The After School Program of John Wesley

John Wesley (1703-1791) is famous as an organizer of small groups which aimed to restore the moral fabric of English society. While he was studying at Oxford, Wesley, his brother Charles, and several other students formed a group devoted to study, prayer and helping the underprivileged. They were labeled "Methodists" by their fellow students because of the way they used rules and a method to go about their religious affairs. From a modern point of view, this is an after school program. Theirs was a group aimed not only at study, but also at effecting social transformation. And, it was not only an extended study program but also an organized effort to restore the church and society through prayer. This is one of the best ways to organize and mobilize people who are concerned with the brokenness of society. Today' church can benefit from following this model.

A PROPOSAL TO THE BOARD
OF CONGREGATIONAL DEVELOPMENT

- *Subject*: Youth Leadership School for Youth Choir and Children Choir
- *Purpose:* In this troubled world, the church faces the issue of life or death. It has ever deepening concerns with loss of membership; some churches are even being forced to close. This proposal outlines new ideas for developing Youth Leadership and enhancing existing leadership. Both can help restore the church.

Therefore, I would like to propose a *Youth Leadership School* to United Methodist Church, Wisconsin Conference. There are still many young people and children at schools in villages and towns who have the capacity for becoming leaders. However, the churches have no means of cultivating their talents. If we are able to do this successfully, the church could grow. Youth and children would bring their parents and friends to church and we would be able to fill it.

Suggested Programs are as follows:

Youth Leadership School:

- *Term*: six months or year programs.
- *Requirements* for developing an educational program which addresses youth ministry in the area of Bible study, music, games, outreach etc.; part-time or full-time.

- *Appointment*: Conference should appoint Youth Ministers to the various churches. At present, this type of leadership is lacking except in some churches.
- *Funding*: This program would be financed by the Conference and local church together.

Organizing Youth Choir

- *Purpose:* To bring young people, parents, and others to the church through the Youth Choir activity.
- *Reward:* Conference and churches need to support scholarships for thoseyoung people who take part in the Music Ministry.
- *How to organize?*: Conference and Circuit should encourage local churches to organize teams which would then develop Youth Choir.

Children Choir/Chrystal Bell Choir: Same direction as Youth Choir.

Vacation Bible School: Many small town churches are not able to open VBS due to lack of leadership. Therefore, they ought to request a special team from a larger, neighboring church and/or a Korean churches to come and lead.

Circuit Revival Worship and Conference

- *Purpose:* This should help the local church to revitalize itself in a spiritual crisis. People need to be awakened to the spirit, to understand *why we need to either rejoice ore repent.* And, they need to know what is going on in America and the world through discussions at the Circuit Conference. The latter provides an opportunity for reflection and can show people how to revitalize the church.
- *How to conduct this workshop*: The Circuit should bring in an impressive guest speaker to outline the agenda and the Annual Conference should provide a forum for discussion on restoring the spirit and the church. This should take place group-by-group with all of the Circuit congregations. All of the churches under the Circuit need to gather together at one point in the same place.
- *When*: Every six months or once a year.

By way of conclusion, we need to recall the work, *Who Moved My Church?* by Mike Nappa. He suggests that "When the church is missing, you'd better go out and find it."[2] Jesus teaches the same thing: "Go out quickly into the streets...There is still room" (Luke 14: 21-22). Yes, we have to go out right away. A lake which has a lot of bait attracts fish. Is there enough tasty bait in the church for people who are hungry and look for spiritual sustenance? The

church people work hard on annual programs: Bazaars, craft shows, bake sales, etc., but these things don't result in an increase in membership. As things currently stand, the church is like a hen which is not able to produce any eggs.

As Nappa also says, "As you know, someone has moved our church, and we are determined to find it for Your sake, Lord. Lead us, guide us, direct us, show us, steer us, conduct us, channel us, point us, funnel us to Thy path. Into Thy hands we commend our spirits. Amen."

It seems hard for today's church to put into practice Jesus' words, "Go out quickly into the streets." Today's church faces a stumbling block when it comes to taking up Nappa's suggestion: "When the church is missing, you'd better go out and find it."

There are three cultures that surround and relate to the church, the American culture, the church culture, and the biblical culture. American culture expresses itself as a sort of multi-culture, a melting-pot and interracial blend. It is nevertheless based on the common ground of equality for all and respect for the common weal. By contrast to this, the Church culture is more like a group or a family. It is based on bloodlines which, by definition, limit outreach to others. Both cultures value privacy. It is given priority where personal and social relationships are concerned. These two cultures sometimes seem to constitute an obstacle to the development of a religious or Biblical culture. The emphasis on privacy does not encourage greeting others or knocking on the doors of neighbors, because it may be perceived as bothersome. However, the Biblical culture is the Kingdom culture. In Jesus' words, "If you greet only your brothers, what are you doing more than others? Do not even pagans do that? (Matt. 5: 47). He practiced the openness associated with the culture of the Kingdom—it was central to his teaching.

The Biblical culture says that all people are one in God. Jesus and his teaching do not therefore merely span human and church culture. Instead, He teaches the Kingdom culture that is based on divine values, and worthiness beyond the worldly culture. For Jesus, everybody is a subject of his ministry, everybody is welcomed at His table, without consideration of bloodline or social status. He reaches out everybody on the streets knocking on doors. And He widened the scope of his mission to include the desert, mountains, villages, houses, streets, etc. Still, today's church leaders confine themselves to church offices and buildings. The streets seem to be foreign to them. They are not familiar with village and town, indeed, they willfully segregate themselves from the world. They know only parishioners and the inside of the church buildings. The result is that they are not at all interested in contact with their community or in reaching out to people on the streets and creating fellowship. The church leader is not a guest and visitor during the term of appointment. He or she is a part of the community and village, the host of the Kingdom table. He or she is not a foreigner in town, but rather a key to transforming the world around him/her. The streets are our parish.

However, the attitude of today's preachers is the polar opposite of what Jesus commanded and also what Nappa[3] suggests. When the church has shrunk, today's pastor reports to Superintendent on the crisis within his church. The Superintendent comes down to check up on the situation like an inspector or insurance agent would. And then he begins to prepare paperwork which will determine whether or not the church closes, instead of trying to help effect a turnaround, instead of going out and bringing people in. This is why the church is now disappearing and may soon be gone. But, people are still in the town. Things are going well everywhere except at the church.

NOTES

1. Young Choe, *Authentic Pastor, Authentic Leadership.* Hamilton Books, Lanham, MD. 2011. See Ch..11; see also p.100 of this work for a more detailed discussion of this issue.
2. Mike Nappa, *Who Moved my Church?* River Oak Publ. Tulsa, OK, 2001. p. 55.
3. Ibid. pp. 40-41.

Chapter Eight

A Concluding Message on Saving the Church

This book has attempted to detect the cause of the decline in the church as well as develop some thinking on how to save it. This is a serious problem in our time. As for the critical issue here, this research began with a range of

questions as part of an attempt to discern the cause and magnitude of this decline. Does the problem point to the end of the Christian era altogether? Or, can we anticipate a turnaround? Is Christianity perhaps taking on a new form? Will there be a new religion after the fall of the Christian church?

There is no doubt that we are facing a new trend in the religious community in America. New religions are filling up the empty places where churches have disappeared. These include Muslims and Buddhists, and even pagan sects, atheistic groups and neo-Nazis. We have no objection to any of these except the neo-Nazis and terrorist groups. Our only concern is the disappearance of the Christian church and its heritage and legacy. Honestly, if it does disappear, how will people cope psychologically, socially, and culturally? Where will we turn if Christianity collapses?

Once, when I was preoccupied with this problem, a friend told me "Don't worry about the future! If one church has gone, you will be appointed to the other church." He was clearly not worried about the decline. In his view, the church is available everywhere, both here and there. In a sense, this is true. *In our time, the church may have disappear, but the pastor will survives until retirement.* I don't worry about the decline or loss of the church as a job center. Rather I am concerned with the church as the body of Christ, given that it struggling and shaking at its foundations. We can never give up the church as a spiritual legacy.

As for the solution to this problem, we have to be aware of current trends. There have been various revolutions in agriculture, industry and information science. Day by day, information technology is bringing about endless changes to human life. Alvin Toffler predicted that the emergent civilization would write a new code of behavior relative to energy, money, and power."[1] This constitutes a wholesale revolution in our form of life: Everything is being tossed around and turned upside down. And, if we cling to our old ways of thinking, the ground could soon collapse out from under our feet. Thus, the new wave of change challenges us to work out a new paradigm for our survival—and to do so while the world is trembling.[2]

There are three types of Renaissance happening in our day. First, there is the fact that the time required for our forming and communicating an idea and possibly having to change it has now been reduced from ten years to ten months, ten days, or ten minutes. The second Renaissance concerns the change from a physical workspace to cyberspace and the third is the knowledge revolution. Today professional life requires practical knowledge and knowledge of one's job as much as it does a college diploma.[3]

Accordingly, we have to recognize that a number of companies and organizations have also declined or even disappeared in our day: Borders Books, Radio Shack, the Green Bay Symphony, etc. Lack of leadership and emasculation of management both make it difficult for organizations to adjust to market tensions and social trends. The decline in the church follows a similar pattern.

We live in a radically changing and often unpredictable world. But, it is time to choose either life or death. It does not seem that we will be able to retain our value and worth in traditional terms. This will requires a fighting spirit, a will to seriously assert oneself. If we want to save the church, we need to develop a new paradigm for it. Starbucks Coffee is different in that it reshaped not only business, but also social life. It provided opportunities for human growth in the midst of business decline. I have already mentioned that Jesus is moving into Starbucks. We can learn something where direction and planning are concerned from its CEO, Howard Schultz.

Do you want to save the church? Or, perhaps a better question is how to do this in the midst of its ongoing destruction? I have outlined twenty-four ideas for restoring it in Chapter Four (Children's Crystal Bell Choir with Youth, Open-Window Church, Talk-Talk Meetings etc.). These look like the traditional programs which we have already developed and unfortunately had to close. They talk about a new direction to reignite the church with a burning flame. But, they will guarantee church growth if we practice them enthusiastically. We will see a miracle sooner or later. It is the same with a medical doctor who heals a serious patient by applying a special medicine and giving him emergency care.

The above ideas will help the existing church and they should also ensure its new growth. The newly cultivated church will be a part of the Christian ministry for the next generation and for the newly emerging immigrant community. However, the existing church still comes first, because it is struggling so drastically. It is like an old car that needs to be traded in. Maybe what is needed is an entirely new one. But who can judge this? Nothing has changed, but the Conference which closes the church based on its own rules. When the church has declined to its final twelve members, it will have to close. This is a financial decision, not a matter of faith. If the roof of a house is leaking, we need to either repair or replace it. The existing church is still worth restoring, because it has people, money, leadership, buildings, etc.

Second, we need to lay down our lives for Jesus' teaching and spirit. He is the Son of God, not a man of the institutional church. Jesus is manifested as the image of God in terms of love and justice in the midst of a miserable world. He was born in a manger identified with the poor and abandoned. He journeyed into the desert so as to discipline himself against evil. He launched the Kingdom of God in an effort to restore our broken world. The substance of the Jesus' movement was worked out in four stages of transformation: Spiritual, personal, the move to discipleship, and finally social change. Jesus confronted traditional Jewish religion and existing political regimes. He stood up and cried out for the oppressed. He never presented himself as a Savior and Messiah, nor did he aim to become an idol or an object of adulation. Instead, he himself took on the role of a revolutionary, seeking emancipate people from misery and to liberate the people from slavery and blindness to the institutional religion which was favored by the existing political regimes.[4] He asked his companions to take up the cross, but most of them turned away from this agonizing journey, except a few women. As Dietrich Bonhoeffer stated, "He is for the other." Jesus laid down his life to fix the broken world. If we wish to worship Him, we need go to the streets right away, because He is there. The today's Jesus is not in the physical church, but on the streets. That is where one finds human agony. This is the way of Jesus from yesterday to tomorrow. However, today's church is far from understanding or conveying the true image of Jesus. If we need to save the church in the midst of its decline, we need to commit to following the authentic Jesus.

Third, the solution is to be attentive to the voice of human suffering. God listens to it, but does the church? God heard the voice of the people in Egypt, and Jesus was no stranger agony from the beginning to the end in his life. He was, and is, deeply concerned with the suffering of people and the tribulations of our world. The both were the subject of his movement.

However, today's church does not attend to this. Racial conflict is worsening on the streets. The police power continue to wield power inhumanly. Racial discrimination is still at high levels and moral standards are diminishing everywhere. An ecological catastrophe is seriously threatening our planet as a result of global warming. The polar ice cap of the Northern hemisphere is disappearing and this itself is contributing in a major way to the environmental crisis. And, the world is being threatened by terrorism almost as if it were a chronic disease. Conflicts between world religions are hardly understandable any longer, since some representatives of major religions routinely resort of violence. Who can cope with all of this?

First of all, if the church is represents human suffering and conveys Jesus' message, it needs to make a moral decision as to how to act in keeping with his teachings. After all, He Himself is the manifestation of human agony. The church has to listen to the voices of those who are suffering today. It does not need to separate itself from it since this ism, in effect, why it came into being in the first place. The awareness of suffering begins with contact with our neighbors and commitment to the church community. Where there is suffering, and even agony, there one finds the church.

It is not only a cultural and social center, not merely intended for fellowship. There is no doubt that it can sometimes be a playground, a place for social and cultural recreation. But it is also a quiet place for meditation and a religious shire which it not soliciting money. It is rather for Thy Will —not ours. Jesus never attended to His will in preference to God's. His agony on the cross was the result of his submission to the divine. Therefore, the church is a place in which to represent the substantial message of Jesus' Kingdom movement, a place for encouraging spiritual transformation. It is a place where the broken world can be repaired and restored. And, it stands for love and justice—here and now. If we don't honor and emulate Jesus' suffering as it was transformative of the world, we are merely worshipping Him as an idol.

Jesus' Kingdom movement begins with the community of and near the church. It is not necessary to start preaching and teaching from some remote point like Latin America, Africa, Asia, and Middle East. Instead, the church needs to listen to the voices of agony that are in and around it. If it fails to attend to the community which surrounds it, then it only makes itself ridiculous. If one member of a family is ill, then the family must give priority to ensuring that he or she is properly cared for. But if the parents try to attend to families other than their own, this is equally ridiculous. Today, some churches travel to foreign countries to carry out their ministry yet they do not give proper attention to their own. So, we need to get our priorities straight. First of all, we should be aware of the suffering and struggles that are going on in our own community and properly attend to them.

There is a metaphor for taking care of our world. If a thief invades your garden or house, what are you going to do? Will you merely wait until he goes away? Or will you call the police immediately? Either way, we have to drive out evil. If we don't, it can take control of our lives, take dominion of our world. Silence in the face of evil amounts to complicity with it. This world will be full of the dancing demons if we simply sit back and remain complacent.

Fourth, the true church of Jesus needs to be emancipated from the emasculating force that the institutional church represents. Jesus never created or even recommended, the institutionalization of His teachings, nor did he argue for the development of a church hierarchy, e.g., the Pope, bishops, and pastors. The early Christian community created apostles, elders, deacons, stewards, and bishops, however, this hierarchical system deteriorated historically and come to be focused on power games and monetary rewards. The institutional church has come to run everything, ostensibly in the name of God. Still, all benefits and profits go from the local churches to the upper levels of the hierarchy. Its budget takes priority over the pastor's salary. And, sometimes, when a church finds itself struggling financially, the pastor is simply moved to another church. But the church itself starts to decline and silently disappears. When that happens, who is the winner? And who is the loser? The church is not, by its very definition, the bishop, the superintendent or even the pastor does not exist in order to sustain them, or generally speaking, to support the institution. It rather stands for the Gospel, and labors to save the world spiritually and socio-politically.

Of course, the institutional church is formally committed to sharing its profits with its smaller members. But, it now seems that the rich gets richer and the poor get poorer. Some people always attend a larger, more affluent church, others always go to a smaller one. But the Kingdom of God is not by appointment only. Such a policy does not practice equality, but rather reflects the prevalence of commercial and capitalist interests in our society—it merely gives disproportionately large shares of the wealth and ever greater opportunities to those who are already rich. To equalized appointments within the church, pastors should be rotated from city to village and vice-versa. As concerns Kingdom appointments, everybody needs experience at all levels and in all positions of leadership. The Superintendent should be sent to a three point church after his term ends. The Christian community is not a place where one can merely get a bigger piece of pizza. It rather is a place of shared and equal opportunity.

Fifth, the Conference of each denomination must not be *his* (the Bishop's) but rather *ours* (the community's). The institutional conference usually has a closed door, not an open one. It is dominated by a few members of the hierarchy where its planning and operations. It only provides a very limited venue for people who wish to participate by sharing their ideas, making suggestions or stating opinions. Thus, it represents vertical power rather than a horizontal distribution of it in, and for the sake of, the ministry. There is no doubt that the Conference possesses a number of brilliant and outstanding leaders. However, this vertical power structure prevents them from expressing their views or effecting any change in the larger institution. The Conference needs to keep an open door so that everybody can be a partner in the church undertakings. The church offers a spiritual feast for everybody, no one should be excluded from it, regarded as a stranger or a mere spectator, or in some way socially disqualified from participating. If the Conference meetings include only bishops and superintendents, then it has become *their* Conference, and is no longer *ours*. If, however, everybody is welcome at the meetings, and allowed to help shape policy through brainstorming, then it is indeed *ours*. There is no reason why the church should have to die, if it is run in this way—free from the burden of excessive and top-heavy administration—it may well survive. In other words, redefining the Conference in this way may just be the key to saving the church.

Finally, we have to explore still further this question of why the church is declining. It is only a trend? Is it impossible to restore it? If so, then is it our responsibility to do so? Or is this trend reflective of a still larger and more frightening move toward the twilight of civilization? I would argue that it is still possible to effect a turnaround in the church, but only if we do the hard work that it will require. Laziness, incompetence, inefficiency, emasculation of leadership, unfaithfulness, irresponsibility, insensibility, lack of vision, etc. —all of these vices need to be corrected if we are to placed ourselves on a straight course again. Unless we do this, we will be find ourselves confronted with a situation of total collapse. The red carpet and stained glass can no longer save the church. The hymns of "Sanctus, sanctus . . . " (Holy, holy . . .) will also not save it. Instead, we need to go forth an both honor and emulate the sufferings of Jesus—to show the true face of Christ to our troubled world.

Steve Jobs was a unique and bold thinker. His claim that we ought to "Think different, stay hungry, stay foolish" may also be helpful advice. It could contribute something further to saving the church.

As the Body of Christ, the church ought to welcome the congregation to Communion, enable their participation in Jesus' movement, and practice continual remembrance of the Lord. But it (the church) must also be understood as a being which is physically and spiritually broken, one which should aim to accomplish Thy Will based on love and justice. The Good Samaritan witnessed to Jesus. So, where does eternal life begin for us? It begins when we care for victims who are thrown into the den of thieves. Jesus was the image of the victim, the care-taker of all who suffer. Oftentimes, Jewish religious leaders turned away from the troubled world. So, where does today's church stand on this question? If the church is victimized as a result of its attempts to rescuing people from difficulties, it is, in fact, manifesting Christ in the world. We want, and need, to see an authentic church, one that does just this.

As long as the church is the body of Christ, we don't need to give up on the march toward the Kingdom of God and the transformation in this world. However, if we do give up, God will replace the church with another—a new civilization will emerge on earth in keeping with the demands of the next age. Both Albert Schweitzer and Arnold Toynbee eloquently predicted the fall of Western civilization. And, Francis A. Schaeffer stated, "Western culture is dying." And then asked "Is the Western church dying too?"[5] I do not want to claim that the church, as one remnant of ancient civilization, is disappearing. No matter what happens, you and I will labor to retain it as the body of Christ.

Jesus predicted that, "The Kingdom of God will be taken away from you and given to a people who will produce its fruit. He who falls on this stone will be broken to pieces, but he on whom it falls will be crushed" (Parable of the Tenants, Matt. 21: 33-44). He continued, saying, "Whoever does not have, even what he has will be taken from him. And throw that worthless servant outside, into the darkness, where there will be weeping and gnashing of teeth. (Matt. 25: 29-30).

The decline in the church is become more intense and more problematic than we could have earlier anticipated, and its disappearance will be dramatic. But many of the church leaders try to deny this trend. Yet, there is no hope if we remain ignorant of this crisis and its true dimensions. In the time of the Old Testament prophets, fraudulent leaders were claiming that everything was going well. This, too was a cover up for the brokenness of their society.

They were not awaiting or searching for the Kingdom of God, but only living in their own egoistically defined world.

Still, we cannot give up on our church as the body of Christ. If we don't say things are impossible, many possibilities will remain open to us and we may be able to turn the church around. The real danger lies either in our viewing the situation as impossible, or in deluding ourselves about its seriousness. If we say that everything is continuing to go well in the midst of this decline, then we are merely being lulled to sleep by fraudulent leadership of succumbing to our own tendencies to self-deception. The decline in the church does not have an external cause, but rather comes from ourselves. Unless we recognize this, we will not be able to act to remedy the problem. So, go! Go out into the streets and also work within the church community! Try to contribute at least something to the resolution of this urgent problem!

If today's pastor is liberated from institutional forces that are pressing upon him, the church will finally make a turnaround.

NOTES

1. Alvin Toffler, *The Third Wave*, William Morrow and Co. NY, NY. 1980. pp. xxii-xxiv.

2. Young J. Choe, *Authentic Pastor, Authentic Leadership*, Hamilton Books, Lanham, MD. 2012. p. 8.

3. Ibid, p. 8.

4. Reza Aslan depicts Jesus as a revolutionary rather than a messiah or Savior. As he notes, Jesus never thought of himself as a messiah. This was how he was portrayed by his disciples and by the early Christian community. See Aslan's work, *Zealot,* Random House, NY, NY. 2013. pp. 164-171.

5. Francis A. Schaeffer, *The Church at the End of the 20th Century*, InterVarsity Press, Ontario, CA. 1970. See back cover page.

Some Thoughts on the Church, Its Mission and Its Future

Edgar Zelle

I believe the Christian Church is in need of a *reformation* and that it will happen only from the bottom up and not from the leadership structure of the church. My thoughts on this are as follows.

Spiritual experiences can only be expressed in terms of the images and within the cultural framework in which they are had. Jesus lived in a culture and had a world view that was vastly different from our own. The role of theology should be to discover the spiritual inspirations which were expressed in the Gospels and then express these truths in terms of our own culture and time.

The most significant change to be noted here is in the world view of 'then' and 'now.' In the time Jesus lived and the Gospels were written, people believed that powerful spiritual beings [gods] lived in some mysterious place or in a heaven, and that they had ultimate control over what happened on earth. Humans had to find a way to please them since they could determine one's destiny on earth and even after death.

This led to a biblical understanding of a universe and a world as created by God, and to the acceptance that we are destined for either heaven or hell after death. How an individual fared eternally depended on 'pleasing the gods.'

Many centuries later, an itinerant preacher by the name of Jesus of Nazareth came to be viewed as "God in made flesh, suffering and dying for the sins of human beings so that those who believe in him might have eternal life." This was a compelling, attractive, comforting theology and the message spread throughout the Roman World. Eventually, Christianity became linked to the ruling powers of the post-Roman Empire and used by them to control their subjects.

This early Christian-era theology of 'heaven/hell' has continued into our time. While it is still comforting and reassuring for people who became familiar with it in their childhood, it has become problematic for many who are interested in recent scientific discoveries which have changed our understanding of the nature and purpose of existence. There are certainly Christians who insist that the Bible is divinely inspired and true as written, and who resist any and all change, but this just doesn't work anymore for many people in the twenty-first century.

When the theology of the church no longer seems relevant to people, they either struggle to find new ways to understand the spiritual realities of the faith or stop participating in the life of a congregation altogether. I strongly believe that, if American Christianity resists change where its theology is concerned, the American Church will succumb to the fate of European churches and become an empty relic of the past.

Where do we go from here? History will ultimately reveal the direction to be taken. The most we can do is to seek new ways to express the spiritual truths of Christianity both in the context of our modern culture and given our current scientific understanding of the universe.

Let's begin with the framework of 'heaven and hell' and a God in heaven who ultimately controls what happens on earth. In fact, we need to relegate these ideas to the past. Our universe is physically much larger than it was understood to be in biblical times and science has proven that human activity has had and is effecting drastic changes in our world; indeed, its effects can 'overpower' the spiritual forces that are present in what we call, nature.

Where our understanding of God is concerned, we are also in need of new images for expressing the divine mystery.

At this point, the question is this: "If Christianity is not about obtaining eternal life in heaven, then what is its meaning for our time?" Theologians have been reflecting on the life of Jesus of Nazareth and a sort of consensus seems to be developing on this, namely, that His spiritual focus was on love—*God's love*—on a God who loves the created world so much that He became incarnate and took on the life of Jesus of Nazareth. Christianity is about how the love of God for his creation, which includes all people and this remarkable earth. Such love transforms our lives and allows us to find peace within, and make peace with others and with the world. Our lives then become a leaven which can further transform society.

On this view, a congregation would be a community which gathers life experience, grows in God's transforming love, and encourages and empowers its members to embody that love in ways that will lead to a more peaceful and just society.

Bibliography

Ahn, Byung-Mu. *Minjungshinhak Iagi: A Story of Minjung Theology*. Seoul. Hankookshinhak Yun-Guso Publ. 1987.
Arias, Esther and Mortimer. *The Cry of My People*. NY, NY. Friendship Press. 1980.
Aslan, Leza. *Zealot*, NY, NY. Random House Publ. 2013.
Bonhoeffer, Dietrich. *Life Together*, Trans. John W. Doberstein, San Francisco, CA. Harper & Row. 1954.
Birch, Bruce. *Let Justice Roll Down*, Louisville, KY. John Knox Press. 1991.
Bloom, Linda. *Good News*. The Woodlands, TX, in "Good News". Nov/Dec.2008.
Boff, Leonardo. *Jesus Christ Liberator*. Maryknoll, NY. Orbis Books. 1978.
Bruinsma, Reinder. "How to became an Authentic Christian Leader," in *Ministry*, Silver Spring, MD. Seventh-day Adventist Publ. July 2009.
Bultmann, Rudolf. *Jesus and the Word*, Trans. L.P. Smith and E H. Lantero, New York: Charles Scribner's Sons, 1958.
Chavez, Mark. *Connections*, Lutheran Church Magazine, Maple Lake: MN, 2015.
Choe, Young J. *Authentic Pastor, Authentic Leadership*, Lanham, MD. Hamilton Books. 2012.
Driver, Christopher. *A Future for the Free Church*, London,UK. SCM Press. 1962.
Dyer, Wayne W. *Wisdom of the Ages*, NY, NY. HarperCollins Publ. 1998.
Engel, Friedrich and Karl Marx, *On Historical Materialism*. Ed. Lewis S. Feuer. NY, NY. Anchor Books. 1959.
Flowers, John & Vannoy, Karen. *10 Temptation of Church*, Nashville, TN. Abingdon Press. 2012.
Fredriksen, Paula. *From Jesus to Christ*, New Heaven, CT. Yale University Press. 1988.
Gannon, James. "There is no normal anymore," in USA Today. December 8, 2009.
Grenfell, John Jr. "The Church's Need for Godly Administration," in "Good News." The Woodlands, TX. Nov/Dec 2008, p. 27-29. This article addresses seven rights of a pastor in the United Methodist Church.
Grillmeier, Aloys. *Christ in Christian Tradition*. NY, NY. Sheed and Ward. 1965.
Hewitt, Steve. *Why the Church Is Dying in America*. In "Christian Computing" magazine. July 2012.
Hiers, Richard H. *Jesus and Ethics: Four Interpretations*. Philadelphia, PA. Westminster Press. 1968.
Johnson W. Douglas & Alan K. Waltz, *Facts & Possibilities: An Agenda for the United Methodist Church*. Nashville, TN. Abingdon Press.1987.
Johnson, Spencer. *Who Moved My Cheese?* G.P. Putnam's Sons. NY, NY. 2002.
Kee, Howard C. *Community of the New Age: Studies in Mark's Gospel*. Philadelphia: The Westminster Press. 1977.

Kelly, J. N. D. *Early Christian Doctrines.* NY, NY. Harper & Row Publ. 1960.
Kennedy, Paul. "American Power Is on the Wane," in *The Wall Street Journal*. Jan 14, 2009.
Kim, Hatae. *A Guide to Philosophy* (in Korean). Seoul: Jongnoseojuk, 1987. This is one of the best introductory college textbooks on philosophy available in Korea.
Kittle, Liza. "UMW Membership Continues Dramatic Decline," in "Good News". The Woodlands, TX. March/April, 2012.
Lambrecht, Thomas A. "Study points out Decline," in "Good News". The Woodlands, TX. July/August, 2015.
Metaxas, Eric, *Bonhoeffer.* Nashville, T. Thomas Nelson. 2010.
Metz, J. *Theology of the World,* NY, NY. Herder and Herder Publ. 1969.
Moltmann, Jurgen. *On Human Dignity.* London, UK/ Minneapolis, MN. Fortress Press. 1974.
Moltmann, Jurgen. *The Crucified God.* (Ch. 6). NY, NY. Harper & Row. Publ. 1974.
Nappa, Mike. *Who Moved My Church?* Tulsa. OK. River Oak Publ. 2001.
Narramore, Clyde M. *Why a Christian Leader May Fall,* Wheaton, IL. Crossway Books. 1988.
Ogletree, Thomas. *Use of the Bible in Christian Ethics.* Philadelphia, PA. Fortress Press. 1983.
Pals, Daniel L. "Religion and Personality: Sigmund Freud," in *Eight Theories of Religion,* Oxford, UK. Oxford Univ. Press, 2006.
Pollard, T. E. *Johannine Christology and the Early Church.* Cambridge, UK. Cambridge Univ. Press. 1970.
Renfroe, Rob. "Good News" in *Good News*. The Woodlands, TX. July/August 2014.
Roark, Dalla M. *Dietrich Bonhoeffer,* Waco, TX. Word Books. 1972
Schaeffer, Francis A. *The Church at the End of the 20th Century.* Downers Grove, IL. InterVarsity Press. 1970
Schultz, Thom & Joani. *Why Nobody Want to Go to the Church.* Carol Stream, IL. Tyndale House Publ. 2013.
Secretan, Lance. "The Spirit of Work," in *Imagine* magazine. Philadelphia: Global Renaissance Alliance.
Shepherd, Massy H. "The Rise of Christianity," in *A Short History of Christianity* by Archibald G. Baker, ed. University of Chicago Press, 1940.
Spong, John S. *A New Christianity for a New World.* San Francisco, CA. Harper and Row Publ. 2001.
———. *Why Christianity Must change or Die.* Harper and Row Publ. San Francisco, CA. 1998.
Starobin, Paul. *After America,* Viking Press. NY, NY. 2009.
Suh, Nam-Dong. "Historical References for a Theology of Minjung," in *Minjung Theology,* Maryknoll, NY. Orbis Books. 1981
Sullivan, Andrew. "Christianity in Crisis," In *Newsweek* magazine. April 2, 2012.
Stumme, Wayne C. "Marxist Thought: Materialistic Understanding of History," in *Christians and the Many Faces of Marxism,* Minneapolis, MN. Augsburg Publishing House. 1984.
Theissen, Gerd. *Sociology of Early Palestinian Christianity,* Trans.from German. Philadelphia: Fortress Press, 1978.
Tillich, Paul. *Systematic Theology.* Vol. I. Chicago, IL. Univ. of Chicago Press. 1951. See Part II. (Being and God.)
The General Board of Discipleship of the United Methodist Church, *Faith 1.* Nashville, TN. 2009.
Thompson, Marianne. *The Humanity of Jesus in the Fourth Gospel,* Philadelphia, PA. Fortress Press. 1988.
Toffler, Alvin. *The Third Wave.* William Morrow and Co. NY, NY. 1980. See p. xxii-xxiv.
VanDenburgh, David. "Conflict Resolution: How to handle a Crisis," in *Ministry,* Silver Spring, MD. Seventh-day Adventist Publ. March 2006.
Walker, Williston. *A History of the Christian Church.* NY, NY. Charles Scribner's 1952.
Walsch, Neale D. "Life," in *Imagine* magazine. Philadelphia, PA. American Library. 2000.
Wiesel, Elie. *Dawn,* Toronto. Bantam Books. 1961.
Williamson, Marianne. *Healing the Soul of America.* NY, NY. Simon & Schuster. 2000.
Zuckerman, Mortimer. "The End of American Optimism," in *The Wall Street Journal,* August 16, 2010.

www.ingramcontent.com/pod-product-compliance
Lightning Source LLC
Chambersburg PA
CBHW051103230426
43667CB00013B/2426